Bread Bonanza

Bake fresh & nutritious continental bread at home

by Sangeeta Gupta

edited & designed by Laxmi Devi

UNICORN BOOKS

Publishers

UNICORN BOOKS Pvt. Ltd.
New Delhi-110002
© Copyright : Unicorn Books Pvt. Ltd.

Distributors
Pustak Mahal, Delhi-110006

Sales Centres

- 6686, Khari Baoli, Delhi-110006, *Ph:* 23944314, 23911979
- 10-B, Netaji Subhash Marg, Daryaganj, New Delhi-110002
  Ph: 23268292, 23268293, 23279900 ● *Fax:* 011-23280567
  E-mail: rapidexdelhi@indiatimes.com

Administrative Office

J-3/16 (Opp. Happy School), Daryaganj, New Delhi-110002
Ph: 23276539, 23272783, 23272784 ● *Fax:* 011-23260518
E-mail: unicornbooks@vsnl.com ● *Website:* www.pustakmahal.com

Branch Offices

Bangalore: 22/2, Mission Road (Shama Rao's Compound),
Bangalore-560027, *Ph:* 22234025 ● *Fax:* 080-22240209
E-mail: pmblr@sancharnet.in ● pustak@sancharnet.in

Mumbai: 23-25, Zaoba Wadi (Opp. VIP Showroom), Thakurdwar,
Mumbai-400002, *Ph:* 22010941 ● *Fax:* 022-22053387
E-mail: rapidex@bom5.vsnl.net.in

Patna: Khemka House, 1st Floor (Opp. Women's Hospital),
Ashok Rajpath, Patna-800004
Ph: 3094193 ● *Telefax:* 0612-2302719
E-mail: rapidexptn@rediffmail.com

Hyderabad: 5-1-707/1, Brij Bhawan, Bank Street, Koti,
Hyderabad-500095, *Telefax:* 040-24737290
E-mail: pustakmahalhyd@yahoo.co.in

I.S.B.N. 81-780-6090-6

Edition : 2005

Printed at: Param Offsetters, Okhla, New Delhi-110020

acknowledgements

Many people have helped me in completing this book. I would not have written this book without my family support, especially my husband – my inspiration.

Thanks to Laxmi Devi, for the final editing and design. My special thanks to www.butlermart.com. who helped me with information and equipment for the shoot that was just right to the beginning bakers. Thanks are due to Invitation Corner, a bakery shop, New Delhi for their co-operation.

To Chandradeep Tiwari, for providing excellent photos. And I am immensely indebted to my publisher, Dr. Ashok Gupta, who has made this dream come true.

contents

Tools
The ingredients
The Science behind bread baking
Troubleshooting

White velvet Batter bread
Cranberry and raisin nut batter bread
Light Wheat batter bread
Orange rye bread with fennel
Oatmeal-prune batter bread
Cornmeal Herb batter bread

Classic Challah Egg bread
Wheat and honey challah egg bread
Challah Cinnamon swirl
Rum Raisin Cinnamon breakfast sweet rolls
The best Hamburger buns
Onion Pretzel
Challah dinner knots

Milk bread
Cornmeal honey bread
Caraway-light rye bread
Granola bread
My raisin bread
Cheese Mini loaves
Winter herb bread

the story of bread

I f you look in Webster's Unabridged Dictionary under *bread*, after the initial definition of it being a "baked dough", you'll find that the second interpretation simply states: "livelihood". The American Heritage Dictionary goes so far as to say that bread is "Food in general, regarded as necessary for sustaining life". In certain Arab dialects in the Middle East – where bread originated – bread is actually referred to as "esh", meaning life. These are some rather powerful descriptions for something as humble as a loaf of bread, but it's true: Bread is one of the most important and prevalent foods of the world, simply put.

The ingredients which go into making a loaf of bread are about as basic and wholesome as you can get: flour, water, yeast and salt. There is no need for fancy or expensive equipment; simply the four essential ingredients and a pair of hands; it is these few ingredients that have literally supported populations. Just think for a minute about the importance of bread in our culture alone. To this day bread is considered the body of Christ in Christian Church, and matzo, one of the truly ancient breads remaining today, is eaten by Jews for religious purposes during Pass over.

Bread has been enjoyed throughout history by almost every culture – from the flatbreads of the Middle East and hearty breads of Europe, to the cornbreads of South and Central America. It has been consumed for its nutritional value, used in religious ceremonies, and has even been used as currency (along with beer) to pay the slaves of ancient Egypt.

Although bread making is much different today, it is traced back more than 10,000 years to the Fertile Crescent, from Syria, Lebanon, Israel, Egypt, and further down the Tigris River to the Persian Gulf. An excavation near the ancient city, Ur, revealed ovens, designed for bread baking, that had been idle for almost 4,000 years.

Bread was not always a loaf, or even baked in an oven for that matter. It's speculated that after learning to grind wheat early civilizations made a gruel or porridge by adding water to their grain and boiling it. This porridge left in the open air, under favourable conditions, began to ferment – the phenomenon of fermentation was undoubtedly discovered by accident. The liquid that surfaced on this early wheat "stew" was also most likely the forerunner of beer; with less water added it became dough-like and formed a bread. Interestingly, the famed Parisian baker, Poîlane, whose sourdough is legendary, refers to his bread as "solid beer".

It was with the Greeks that bread began to be thought of as not just part of their diet, but also as an art form. According to food historian Jean-Françoise Revel, the Greeks had seventy-two varieties of breads. They are the people credited with refining the art and science of leavening dough and baking bread; they were thought to be such masters that almost all of the bakers of ancient Rome were Greeks. And during the Christian Era, bread was so revered that Jesus taught his followers to pray: "give us this day our daily bread".

In due course of time, bread baking became somewhat stabilised with the use of natural starters which contained wild yeast. As the yeast in starters consumes the natural sugars and proteins in the flour, it gives off gases – mainly alcohol and carbon dioxide – and a distinctly sour smell. Hence the name *sourdough*. Think of it this way: commercial yeast has only been available for a little more than a century, prior to that any bread, or bread product, which was intended to rise, was dependent on wild or natural yeast.

Sourdough is the oldest and original form of leavened bread. The French refer to it as *pain au levain*, and the Italians *pane lievito naturale*, both translating roughly to leavened bread. And when the early settlers from Europe landed in America, they were carrying with them their cherished sourdough starters. Even Christopher Columbus is said to have had a crock of sourdough aboard his vessel when he first landed on North America.

Later, yeast was being produced commercially. Gradually baking methods improvised. And often bread was baked in a gold dust pan or an empty tin can by pushing it close to an open fire. There was an even more primitive method to cook bread. It was referred to as "stick baking". They would take a piece of firm sourdough, wrap it around the end of a stick and cook it directly over an open fire!

These days, even purists will spike their starters and/ or dough with commercial yeast to give it a boost.

These days, even purists will spike their starters and/or doughs with commercial yeast to give it a boost. It helps create a lighter bread that you'll probably be more accustomed to, but it will still have that distinctively complex sourdough flavour. Also, it will make the sourdough process almost foolproof. As long as you feed the starter twice a week and spike it with a pinch of yeast every month or so, you will have your sourdough starter for years, literally.

The story of bread may be an old one, but the modern truth is that bread is good and good for you. So, the next time you are about to bite into some fresh bread, remember, it's not just a slice of bread in your hand, it's a slice of history.

indian breads

Indian cooking is the fusion of the West and the East, in the most delicate and subtle ways. Not only the history but the religion (from Hinduism to Judaism) and the foreign invasions and its culture have influenced so much that we now have created the spectacular palette of foods we know as Indian cuisine.

Bread is one example. Previously, Indians didn't know of any bread that rose above a couple of centimeters after being cooked. The Portuguese were one of the first to bring to India yeast, which produced the loaves of bread. The Indians dubbed these new breads the double roti or "double bread".

Otherwise, Indians eat flat bread. Call it nan, chapatti, poori or paratha, it is bread. India boasts of a variety of breads, most of which are flatbreads, except for poori, which arrives as a big round puff after having been deep-fried.

Varieties of Indian breads are:

Mooli Paratha: Paratha stuffed with spiced radish mixture and roasted with a good helping of pure ghee.

Sheer-mal: A rich bread with a Persian influence made with a helping of milk, khoya etc. and sprinkled with poppy seeds on top.

Rajasthani Bati: A typical Rajasthani bread made of whole wheat flour and ghee.

Luchi: Miniature version of the puri – Bengali style.

Nargisi Puri: A rich puri with egg and potato stuffing.

Bermi Puri: Puri made of dal and spices, a Jodhpur speciality.

Indori Palak Puri: Indori style deep fried puri with spinach and spices.

Batata Puri: A Potato variation of the common puri.

Gobi Paratha: Thick parathas stuffed with grated cauliflower filling.

Bhatura: A thick puri deep fried in oil, a very good accompaniment for the Punjabi chhole.

Missi Roti: A variation of the famous roti, made of refined flour and spinach – simply delicious.

Roomali Roti: A truly fine roti which is cooked on an 'ulta tava'.

Methi Puri: A tasty puri from North India made with Fenugreek leaves.

Kashmiri Puri: A simple puri made of yeast, curd and spices.

Dalbhari Puri: A variation of the common puris – these are stuffed with mixed dals and then deep-fried.

Tandoori Roti: A style of roti/pancakes prepared from refined flour and egg and then baked in a tandoor.

Mint-stuffed Parathas: Pancakes made of whole wheat flour, mint sauce and stuffed with cabbage, peas and potato.

Methi ki Roti: Fried roti stuffed with methi (fenugreek leaves).

Stuffed Masala Kulcha: Indian roti stuffed with a paneer-potato mixture.

Makai ki Roti: Wholesome pancakes made from fresh maize flour served with a lot of ghee.

Puri: Deep-fried puffed bread.

Aloo Paratha: Shallow-fried unleavened bread with a tangy potato stuffing.

Pudina Paratha: Mint-flavoured unleavened bread.

Roti/chapatti: It is a basic bread prepared from whole wheat flour, and forms the staple diet of the Indians.

Naans: Triangles of refined flour and egg dough traditionally baked in a clay oven.

Methi Thepla: Fenugreek-flavoured unleavened Indian bread.

The Portuguese were one of the first to bring yeast to India, which produced the loaves of bread.

the challenge of learning 'how to bake'

any of you buy Continental breads from the bakery.

But have you tried making them on your own? Before saying 'yes', forget that baking Continental bread is a very difficult and tough task. Be positive and explore the world of baking Continental breads. Alone in your kitchen, you will find that the process of making a yeasted dough and baking your own bread is not only a scientific and experimental craft but also a gastronomical exhilarating experience.

Be assured that your bread will be far better than those mass-produced loaves in a factory. Your loaves will have their own *character*, *flavour* and *distinctive appearance*. The only difference between a good baker and you is *practice*. While making and baking the dough, you will experience the satisfaction of creating something new every time. But this doesn't hold true in every situation. No doubt, initially some loaves might look different from what they should look, but just remember, how many maps of different countries have been drawn while making *chapattis* as a beginner and everyone had a good laugh too! Through practice you can improve each loaf over the previous one. So, why not give it a try?

The first time a baker would face initial hiccups are like:

1. *Did I make the proper mix?*
2. *Was I kneading correctly?*
3. *Were my baking temperatures correct?*
4. *Would the yeast bubble?*
5. *Would my baked bread turn out to be BREAD; brown, crisp, golden, dome-shaped delicious bread?*

But towards the way of becoming a good and an experienced baker, you will be faced with many challenges and some unanswered questions. But it's a wrong myth that bread making is a very cumbersome task. Many people have given up after the initial try. But if you read this book carefully, it will be able to resolve all your teething problems while trying each recipe.

So, from where should the amateur begin?

> It's a wrong myth that bread making is a very cumbersome task. Many people have given up after the initial try. But if you read this book carefully, it will be able to resolve all your teething problems while trying each recipe.

The amateur baker can begin with the most basic loaves that are quite simple to make. There are some master recipes wherein one can make a wide variety of breads from each type of dough. The recipes described in the book in a step-by-step sequence are intended to act a a foundation, which can be transformed into infinite variations, once the basic skill have been mastered. Each recipe also has several variations with different flavours and textural elements.

This book will not only guide you about the recipes but also enthuse in you the confidence to invent your own recipes. When you have tried the recipes from this book, you will have a vast knowledge of breads and baking skills and al tampered with your own pattern of break making.

Understand the world of baking. Always keep in mind these basic principles of baking:

- Proper measurements
- Appropriate kneading
- Rising temperature and time
- Baking temperatures and
- Correct baking time.

The key words of baking are *time* and *temperature.*

BEGIN at the first BREAD RECIPE – Yeasted Batter Bread Apply all the principles of yeast baking without the kneading and long-rising times. The only thing you require is *vigorou. beating,* just as if you were making "Dahi Bhalla" or a "Cake" With the minimal effort, you will be able to make tasty, high quality bread with a coarse crumb and rough top crust that will slice beautifully.

A good loaf must meet the following criteria:

- Easy to assemble and mix
- Minimal clean-up
- Predictable rising time
- Nutritional ingredients
- Symmetrical dome-shaped loaf
- Moist texture with a hair-thin brown crust
- Sweet grain-rich smell
- Easy to slice
- Delicious flavour

How to use this book?

- First read the recipe and make a list of ingredients that are required for baking a bread.
- Assemble your ingredients and equipment to set up your workstation.
- Review the recipe to double check the timing, equipment and ingredients and then set to work.

While baking you will be acquainted with the complex beer-like-smell associated with the raw dough and also the aroma of the finished loaf. This sensory basis will enable you to analyse and develop your own criteria for tasty and good-looking loaves. By using your cooking instincts and senses; improving through trial and error – are the keys to perfecting a recipe, thereby becoming a good baker. Remember to follow your instincts. The technical skills will be acquired along the way. And, of course, don't panic, be confident, relaxed and enjoy the process.

baking school

A re you ready to make your first loaf? Before you try, read this section, because it provides all the necessary information imparted in a baking class. This is from where you need to begin and understand, before proceeding to the recipe. READ about the tools, check what you already have and make a note of what you will need. Then review the ingredients, since they form the basis of good dough. Flour and Yeast are the star ingredients in any recipe, hence obtaining the right quality and quantity of these ingredients is of utmost importance. Finally, the technique should be carefully read. Some techniques might be familiar and others might seem new. This section presents all the required basics that can be used as shaping a loaf to baking.

The tools

You don't need a lot of fancy equipment to make bread. If you cook on regular basis, you probably have all the essentials on hand – an extra mixing bowl, heavy-duty electric stand mixer, measuring cups and spoons, a long-handled wooden spoon, a bread pan, an oven, and the most important, your hands!

Over a period of time, these tools have been improvised both, with regard to shape and materials like use of silicon-coated heavy-gauge aluminium, heat absorbing black steel, glass pans, resulting in convenience and better quality baking. All the tools required are available in cookware shops, well-stocked grocery stores and departmental stores.

Bakeware

Every baker has different bakeware preferences ranging from heavy aluminium, European tin, ovenproof glass, and earthenware to non-stick silicone. Pans give form to loaves that may not be strong enough to hold their own shape. There are different sizes and shapes of moulds available in the market, but loaf pans and baking sheets are used more often.

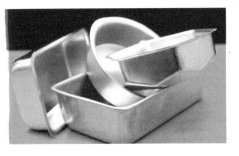

Loaf pans, which make the standard regular sandwich style loaf of bread, come in several sizes. **Heavy-gauge aluminium**, often with a silver non-stick coating, is lightweight, inexpensive, easy to clean, and the best conductor of heat for baking, since the material responds quickly to changes in heat. The gauge or thickness of the pans determines their efficiency in reflecting heat. Compared to lightweight pan, a professional heavyweight aluminium pan is less likely to warp (twisted from its original shape) or develop hot spots.

Avoid **stainless steel**, as it does not efficiently conduct heat. **Black tinned steel** is a good conductor of heat but scratches easily, reacts to acidic foods and rusts quickly if not washed and dried properly.

If you have your grandmother's **aluminium spice-container** (a circular-box with containers to keep different spices) stored somewhere, then it can also be used to bake small, beautiful cup-shaped loaves.

Nowadays, **tin moulds** made of baking sheets are used for baking. Being quite heavy at base, they lead to uniform rising and baking.

Disposable aluminium foil pans are easily available in the market in different sizes. They can be placed directly on a baking surface. They bake a beautiful loaf of bread and can be washed for reuse.

Pyrex glass loaf pans are non-reactive and good conductors of heat, and brown loaves faster than aluminium. Moreover, glass being transparent, remember to keep a watch on the loaf, while baking.

Disposable aluminium foil pans

Glass loaf pans are perfect for baking sticky sweet breads like cinnamon swirls. **Ceramic loaf pans** are easily available, and they make wonderful loaves of bread. Whether glazed or unglazed on the inside, they are heavy, slow and steady conductors of heat. Sugary dough should not be baked in such pans as they stick to the porous clay and ruin the pan for subsequent baking. So, always place clay pans on the lowest oven racks for the bottom of the loaves to brown properly. Generally, it takes about ten minutes longer to bake a loaf in a clay pan than in a metal pan. These pans are easily washable with the help of sponge and soap water.

Baking Sheets

Another piece of essential bakeware is a good baking sheet. Look preferably for the heaviest gauge aluminium or tin-plated steel, which don't wrap. Perforated baking sheets are great for crusty country breads. And ceramic

baking sheets are best for Focaccia (Italian breads). The size of the oven will dictate the size of the baking sheet. Make sure to use baking sheets that are a few inches smaller than your oven so that it allows for adequate heat circulation.

Cooling Racks

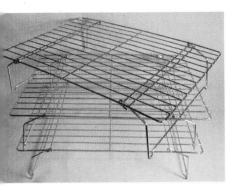

Hot breads just out of the oven need to be transferred to a raised stainless steel wire or wooden rack on the counter to make the crust crisp. Cooling on the rack allows air to circulate all around the loaf, especially on the bottom, and prevent the evaporating steam from turning the bread into an uneven, soggy loaf. Usually, such a rack is provided in the oven, for grill purposes.

You can use even those steel or aluminium circular racks (about six inches in diameter), which are placed beneath the pans containing boiling or very hot materials, kept usually on table top or kitchen shelf-top.

Dough Scrapers

Dough scrapers, also known as bench knives or dough cutters, are 6×3 inches in size, flexible, rectangular plastic cards used to scrape bowls and cutting dough into portions. They are quite useful for transferring soft dough and stretching dough during kneading.

They also come in stainless steel, called bench knife scrapers with either a plastic, wooden or steel-capped handle.

Mixer

Bread dough can be mixed either *by hand* or a heavy-duty *electric stand mixer.* Hand-held mixers do not have the power to mix bread dough. So you can use stationery mixers designed for this purpose. They make mixing enjoyable and can efficiently handle small, medium and large quantities of dough with ease, especially when the dough requires vigorous mixing and kneading. The mixers have either a dough hook attachment or mixing blade that is designed to replicate hand kneading. Usually you begin mixing with the paddle attachment and then switch to the dough hook when the dough thickens. You may have to stop the machine from time to time to add flour.

Knives

Bread should always be cut with a stainless steel, serrated knife to avoid tearing the beautiful, tender interior and breaking the crust. A simple knife drags the bread with itself while cutting, resulting in untidy slices or portions. Such a knife is also useful for cutting sweet roll dough portions or slashing decoratively before baking. Even a dough scraper or a pizza cutter is quite useful for cutting and edging dough; portioning and cutting baked flat breads. A kitchen shear or a pair of scissors is also required in some type of breads.

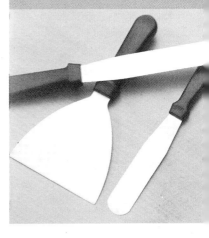

Bread dough can be mixed either *by hand* or a heavy-duty *electric stand mixer.* Hand-held mixers do not have the power to mix bread dough. So you can use stationery mixers designed for this purpose.

Measuring cups and spoons   *Mixing Bowls*

Measuring Cups and Spoons

Getting the right amount of ingredients is vital to baking good bread. Measuring cups and spoons both for dry and liquid ingredients should be kept close at hand.

Mixing Bowls

There are various types of mixing bowls like plastic, steel, glass or ceramic, available in the market. Though the type of bowls doesn't affect the quality of the bread, but ceramic bowls are preferred over others. Being heavy, they do not topple around while you are mixing the ever-stiffening dough. Always match the bowl size with your mixing implements – too small a whisk or spoon will just not do the job.

Oven

This is an appliance you as a baker can't do without. You find different options in ovens like conventional, electric and gas ovens, fan-forced convection ovens and microwaves. If you have a small oven, make sure your pans fit comfortably in it with enough space all around and between the loaves for proper heat circulation; otherwise, bake one loaf at a time. *Conventional ovens* have the heating element on the bottom of the oven floor, while *convection ovens* have circulating heat, which allows for baking on several racks at one time. Breads bake more quickly in convection ovens, so lower the temperature by 10 degrees Celsius. *Microwave ovens*, which

Microwave ovens, which convert electricity into microwave energy, are not good for baking yeast breads. They are best used for gentle reheating and for direct method, which speeds up the traditional slow rise time by half.

convert electricity into microwave energy, are not good for baking yeast breads. They are best used for gentle reheating and for direct method (explained in detail later on), which speeds up the traditional slow rise time by half. In our country, usually two types of ovens are preferably used for home baking – the Oven-Toaster-Griller (OTG) and the oven incorporated in the cooking ranges.

Plastic Rising Buckets

Though bread dough can be raised in all sorts of bowls, a long narrow and heavy *acrylic rising bucket* with a lid is preferable. The dough rises vertically in such a bucket, which makes a better dough, rather than rising in a wide bowl, and is easy to handle. Besides, a transparent container also provides better visibility in observing how much the dough has risen.

Parchment Paper

Silicone-coated parchment paper or baking paper is essential for a baker's kitchen. It is the best way to make a baking pan non-stick and cut down on cleaning. Do not substitute writing or brown paper for baking purposes, as it might be made from recycled paper, and inedible. It also might be toxic, since chemicals are mixed with the pulp.

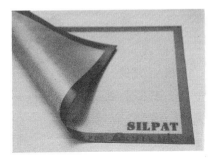

Oven Mittens

The mittens are a must to protect the hands while handling the hot pans and trays. They are available in different varieties and should be extra large and quite thick so as to protect the wrists and lower arms.

Plastic Wrap

Keep a roll of cellophane or plastic wrap in the widest width available. The plastic wrap is used to cover the dough, during different stages of rising.

Pastry Brushes

A pastry brush should be a natural bristle brush, preferably 1 to 3 inches wide. It is used for applying glazes and brushing sweet dough with butter, as well as for dusting excess flour off the workspace. The soft bristles do not damage or deflate risen dough. One or two brushes of different width will serve the purpose.

Scale

Beam-balance, electronic or spring scales are used for weighing ingredients, such as flour, fruits and nuts. Having a scale is optional, since cups and spoons can also be used for measuring and weighing purposes. It is only when baking is done on a large scale, or when many loaves are to be made that having a scale might become essential.

Spatulas

Rubber spatulas are necessary for scraping batter from the sides of a mixing bowl, the work bowl of an electric mixer, for scraping accumulated dough of the dough paddle, and turning dough out of the rising bucket. Even spoonulas, the spatula with a slightly curved paddle or hook, comes quite handy while transferring batters. A rolling pin and a small mesh strainer are also useful while rolling out dough.

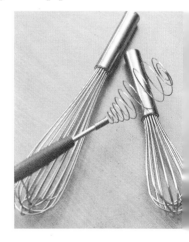

Rubber **spatulas** are necessary for scraping batter from the sides of a mixing bowl.

Timer

Time plays a vital role, from making the dough, to rising, to baking the dough. A timer, be it the turn-and-set, the dial type or a digital one, is a fool proof tool for keeping track of everything from proofing yeast to rising and baking time. Even if you do not have a timer, keep a watch nearby and keep track of the time by writing down time against each process, on a piece of paper.

Whisks

Stainless steel wire whisks, with either a metal or a wooden handle, are quite useful while making the dough. The small ones are quite useful while beating egg glazes and powdered sugar glazes and fillings. The balloon wire whisks and the Danish dough whisks are great for beating yeast batters.

Thermometer

Use thermometer to accurately gauge the temperature of your liquid ingredients, dough or finished loaf. And it is available in all cookware shops.

Since the activity of yeast is quite sensitive to temperature, accurately gauge the temperature of your liquid ingredients, dough or finished loaf by using a long-stemmed instant read yeast or digital probe thermometer. To read, just insert the stem and read the temperature. Loaf bread will register 90 to 95 degrees Celsius when baked to perfection. Every oven bakes at a slightly different temperature. An old-fashioned oven thermometer is also useful. It is necessary to be certain that the interior of the oven is at a temperature you have set and that it is holding to that temperature.

Work Space

You need an easy-to-clean, smooth work surface for hand kneading, portioning and shaping dough. This can be a hardened board, a slab of marble or a plastic chopping board about 15 × 21 inches in size. Each type of board has its own merits and demerits. A wooden board gives friction, a marble one is smooth to work on, and a plastic one (with a towel underneath to prevent slipping) is easy to clean. Even the stainless steel circular bowl (*'parat'* in Hindi) used for kneading flour while making chapattis can be used, provided it is big. A small bowl would hamper mixing and kneading movements. Leave plenty of room around the workspace for unrestricted and easy arm movements. There should also be ample space to keep containers of ingredients required, like flour, sugar, salt and yeast.

26

The common ingredients used in bread-making are:

- Flour
- Yeast
- Salt
- Sweeteners
- Fats

Flour

Flour is the primary ingredient in bread and the type of flour used in the recipe will determine the nature of the flour. Today, bread is almost always made of wheat but in the past rye, barley, oats, rice and maize (often called Indian corn until recently) were used or mixed. (Corn and rye, of course, are still used occasionally.) Everybody knows it is wheat flour that yields the best bread. Because only wheat flour contains protein-forming component called gluten, a substance that supplies the structure needed for leavening. Generally, there are two types of wheat flour used in making bread loaves, *whole-wheat flour* and *all-purpose flour (maida)*. Flour needs to be sifted while making the dough. Other specialty flours such as corn, rye, semolina, oats, and gram can also be mixed in small proportions (about 30%) with wheat flour for nutritional flavoured loaves. Slowly and gradually you will be able to recognise different kinds of flour by sight and by feel. Bread flour and all-purpose flour are creamy white and slightly coarse to touch. Stone-ground whole-wheat flour is coarse and gritty, whereas finely ground whole-wheat flour is quite smooth and pale brown in colour. One thing to keep in mind is to avoid mixing an old batch of flour with a

> Wheat flour yields the best bread because it contains protein-forming component called gluten, a substance that supplies the structure needed for leavening.

fresh one. Each flour absorbs a different amount of moisture and at a different rate; hence small variations will surely occur every time you take a batch of flour. More the non-wheat flour (corn, oats etc.) you use in proportion to wheat, the denser is the loaf and slower is the rising time.

Some Types of Flour

Cornmeal Flour (made from Maize, मक्का)

Cornmeal flour is used to make yeasted corn bread. It can be ground, both fine to coarse. To get best flavour, search out for fresh stone-ground flour available at your nearby local mill and store it in the refrigerator, to preserve it. Usually fresh cornmeal flour is available in the winter season.

Bread Flour

Bread flour is high in gluten content and thus results in bread with good volume. Dough made with bread flour should be kneaded longer than dough made from all-purpose flour.

Millet Flour (*Bajra*, बाजरा)

Millet grain is tiny, round and yellow in color, and resembles pale mustard seeds. It has a slight nutty taste and a fluffy texture. It is easy to digest and is very nutritious.

Oat Flour (जई)

Oats may be ground into oat flour, resulting in a mild, nutty flavour. Tinned oat flour is also available in the market. Honey, nuts, spices and other dry fruits can also be added to the dough to enhance the flavour of the bread.

Rice Flour (चावल)

Rice flour can be ground from brown or white rice. Bakers mostly prefer brown rice flour because it is an excellent thickener, and is good for dusting, as it absorbs moisture slowly. It also has a light sweet flavour.

Rye Flour (राई)

It has a characteristically strong, earthy flavour and contains a small amount of gluten. Often the flavour of rye is enhanced by a small amount of vinegar. Limited in gluten content, it is combined with all-purpose, whole-wheat or bread flour to improve volume and texture. You can substitute *kutu* or *singhara* flour for rye flour.

Shredded or broken Wheat Bread (*Daliya*, दलिया)

Breads made of shredded wheat are an excellent source of nutrition and good for the stomach. It is also used with milk to make porridge. Shredded wheat bread tastes good, is easily digested and is beneficial for children and old persons. Flour need not be sifted while making bread.

Yeast

Yeast is a fungus form of plant life, consisting of minute cells, which grow and multiply at blood heat if fed with sugar and moisture. It is rich in vitamin B.

Today bread is leavened with yeast. Yeast is used in baking to ferment sugars present in the flour or added to the dough. It eats the sugar and complex carbohydrates in the flour and the carbon dioxide gets trapped in the stretchy mesh-like structure of the dough in the process of rising and fermentation.

Yeast not only performs its leavening function but also produces many other chemical substances that flavour the baked product and change the dough's physical properties. Remember, yeast responds to favourable conditions like moisture and warmth. Moisture causes the yeast to begin formation and stimulates gluten. Moisture is supplied by water, milk, buttermilk, or yogurt, sour cream or cottage cheese, potato water (water in which the potatoes have been boiled in), beer (at room temperature), wine, fruit juice or cider (fermented drink made from apple juice), or a combination of any of these.

> Remember, yeast responds to favourable conditions like moisture and warmth.

29

Sour milk can also be used. To make sour milk, add the juice of half a lemon or one teaspoon cider vinegar to a cup of fresh milk. Each liquid used will provide a distinct flavour and taste to the bread. A loaf made with water has a heavy, crisp crust and a chewy texture. Milk gives a light even texture and a thin brown crust, and the added fat keeps the bread fresh for a longer period. A combination of milk and fat makes the bread tender. Even the type of water used affects the quality of bread. Hard water is alkaline, weakens the gluten and makes a loaf with less volume. Soft water being acidic makes the yeast more active. It is best to use spring or bottled water.Unless it is raw, the milk need not be boiled and cooled. Boiling eliminates the presence of enzymes that might sour and slacken the gluten. Even dry milk powder can be used mixing it with water. If the dough ends up too dry, sprinkle it with some water and knead again, or float a section of the dough in a bowl of water, and knead in the soaked mass.

Types of Yeast

There are five types of yeast:

- Active dry yeast
- Instant dried yeast
- Compressed fresh cake yeast
- Quick rise yeast
- Bread machine yeast

To make the yeast active, make a mixture of water, a pinch of sugar and yeast. This step is called 'PROOFING'. Generally, for about 1 kilogram of flour, about 2-3 teaspoons of yeast is needed. The season, in which the bread is made, also influences the amount of yeast to be taken. In summers, 2 teaspoons (for 1 kg of flour) is sufficient, but in winters, 3 teaspoons might be needed as dough rises slowly due to lack of heat.

Of the different types of yeasts available, active dry and fresh cake yeast are usually used for baking at home. The other types of yeast are more suited for commercial purposes, where a large volume of baking is done. Even the fresh cake yeast is less suited for baking at home since it is highly perishable and even when refrigerated, lasts for only about two weeks.

Active Dry Yeast

It was developed keeping stability in mind and has a larger grain size than other dry yeasts. Dry yeasts are not activated (consider them as little plants asleep) until proofed. It is to be dissolved in about 1/4th cup of lukewarm (40-45 degrees Celsius) liquid. Having a yeast thermometer will certainly help in accurately ascertaining the temperature of water. Another way of gauging the temperature of water is to sprinkle a few drops of water on the inside of the wrist or at the back of the palm as is done while checking the temperature of the milk in the baby bottle. The water must feel warm; neither too hot nor too cold. If the water is too cold, the yeast will be slow to activate or even might not activate at all. If the water is too hot, the yeast might be killed. In both the cases, dough will not rise properly. The yeast should be considered dead if the characteristic foaming and bubbling do not occur within ten minutes of mixing it with liquid.

Always keep dry yeast in an airtight container in the refrigerator. It tends to spoil if left open. Dry yeast gets oxidised, when it comes in contact with air. Active dry yeast, once opened, should be used within 3 months for optimum rising power. To be on the safe side, it is always better to poof your yeast if there has been a long gap since your last baking. While purchasing yeast, do remember to look at the expiry date on the packet.

Yeast is a living micro-organism. It produces carbon dioxide gas from the sugars that are present in the dough. Apart from carbon dioxide gas several other aromatic substances and flavour compounds are formed.

Instant Dried Yeast – Fast Acting Yeast

Also called fast acting yeast, it comes from Belgium. It is dried to a very low percentage of moisture and coated with ascorbic acid and a form of sugar, which enables the yeast to activate immediately on contact with warm liquid. Like dry yeast, which requires some sugar or starch to activate properly, fast acting yeast does not require any sugar to activate. It also does not need initial proofing and can be directly added to the dry ingredients as in the rapid mix method, explained later.

Fast acting yeast contains three times as many yeast cells by volume; hence it should be used about 25% less than active dry yeast and $1/3^{rd}$ the amount of fresh cake yeast in a recipe. After opening the vacuum packet, store the yeast in an airtight container in the freezer to prevent oxidation. Fast acting yeast can be stored upto one year.

Compressed Fresh Cake Yeast

This type of yeast is known for its dependability, excellent rising ability and superior flavour as compared to dry yeast strains. It is available in cakes of various sizes weighing up to 200 gms. Smaller cakes, weighing 25 gms., to be used at home, are stabilised with starch to prolong shelf life, but this tends to decrease its potency.

Fresh cake yeast is highly perishable, and remains active for only about two weeks; hence it is mostly preferred for commercial purposes. When fresh, it is a crisp, even, tan-grey cake with no discolouration and breaks with a clean edge. If the cake of the yeast is soggy and does not break with a sharp crackling sound, you need to use a fresh cake of yeast. Compressed fresh cake yeast should be dissolved in warm liquid, about 35 degrees Celsius, before being added to the dry ingredients. You can substitute fresh cake yeast for active dry yeast in any of the recipes.

Quick Rise Yeast

It is another strain of low moisture yeast that raises dough 50% faster than regular dry yeast. It works best when added directly to the dry ingredients and with liquids standing at about 50-55 degrees Celsius. Due to the yeast's fast fermentation, there is a slight loss of flavour and quality in the finished loaves.

Bread Machine Yeast

It is finally granulated and coated with ascorbic acid and a flour buffer to make it stable enough to be mixed directly with the flour and other dry ingredients before the liquid is added. It is not as sensitive as active dry yeast to temperature changes. Of all the types of yeasts, **active dry yeast** is easily available in the market. Moreover, due to its longer storage life, it is generally preferred for use, by home bakers. Storage and quality points of yeast:

- It should be wrapped and stored in the refrigerator
- Use it as quickly as possible after purchasing, preferably within 7 days. For this reason, it is best bought in small quantities
- It should be fresh and moist, have a pleasant smell and crumble easily
- Remove from chiller before use and use at room temperature
- Yeast requires sugar to ferment
- Proving temperature is best between at 21-32°C, depending on recipe
- The temperature range of liquids used in the making of dough/dissolving of yeasts should be 36-38°C
- Salt retards its properties and can destroy it
- Temperatures above 50°C destroy yeast (but it can start to die above 40°C)
- Yeast can withstand low temperatures without damage

Of the different types of yeasts available, **active dry** and **fresh cake yeasts** are usually used for baking at home.

Salt

Salt brings out the mixed flavours in bread. Though optional, it is considered an essential ingredient for its ability to accentuate other tastes. Salt also acts as a stabiliser so that yeast does not over-ferment. There is usually a ratio of one-teaspoon salt per tablespoon of yeast.

Salt also helps to condition and toughen the protein strands so that they do not break during the rising process, enabling the dough to expand smoothly.

It should be used with care, as too much of salt leaves a bitter taste and can also inhibit the yeast activity. On the other hand, lack of salt results in a flat taste in the finished loaf.

Sweeteners

Some sort of sweetener is usually needed to act as a food for yeast and to give a better flavour and taste to the finished loaf. The amount of sweetener also determines how dark the crust will be. There are various types of sweeteners like granulated sugar, brown sugar, honey, molasses (syrup from raw sugar) and barley malt. While many loaves contain no sugar, some have 1 or 2 tablespoons per 2 cups of flour, with sweet breads having upto 3 to 4 tablespoons per cup.

Too much sugar retards the yeast, hence the sweet dough takes a longer time to rise or to compensate, and more yeast might have to be used while proofing. To substitute honey and other liquid-based sweeteners for granulated sugar, use 3/4th cup honey for each cup of sugar, and reduce the total liquid used in the recipe by 1/4th cup.

Liquid sweeteners are more concentrated in flavour than granulated ones. When using liquid sweeteners, it would be better to slightly oil your spoon or cup, to allow the liquid to flow freely without sticking. Avoid sugar substitute like unfined yellow sugar powder ('*boorha*' in Hindi), as they can't hold the heat and tend to give a bitter chemical aftertaste.

Naturally sweet flours, such as oat, barley reduce or eliminate the need for sugar. Barley, malt, sweet syrup made from the toasted and dried wholegrain, is similar to molasses and a wonderful sweetener for bread.

Fats

Though, in today's modern world, many persons tend to avoid fats and its products. Use of little butter, nuts, olive or vegetable oils in dough imparts flavour, a good moist texture and a rich taste to the bread. They also lubricate the protein meshwork helping in smooth rising of the dough and increasing volume.

Fats also act as a natural preservative, retarding staling of the bread. For good flavour and cholesterol free diet, you can use oils such as Olive, Canola, Soya, Sesame and Sunflower. For two cups of flour, one teaspoon of fat needs to be used.

The Science Behind Bread Making

Bread is the product of baking a mixture of flour, water, salt, yeast and other ingredients. The basic process involves mixing of ingredients until the flour is converted into a stiff paste or dough, followed by baking the dough into a loaf. There are no fancy or difficult steps here. Before you begin:

- Carefully read the recipe.
- Check all the ingredients required.
- Assemble the equipment you will need.
- And finally, follow the steps given below.

Each recipe is broken down into the following steps:	
Step 1:	Mixing the Dough
Step 2:	Rising (fermentation)
Step 3:	Kneading
Step 4:	Dough rising
Step 5:	Deflating the dough
Step 6:	Shaping the dough and final rise
Step 7:	Glazing
Step 8:	Baking
Step 9:	Cooling
Step 10:	Reheating and home freezing

Step 1

Mixing the Dough

Mixing fulfils two functions: evenly distribute the various ingredients and allow the development of a protein (gluten) network to give the best bread possible. Each dough has an optimum mixing time, depending on the flour and mixing method used.

Too much mixing produces dough that is very extensible with reduced elastic properties. Under-mixing may cause small-unmixed patches, which will remain unrisen in the bread. This will give a final loaf with a poor appearance inside. The dough can be mixed by hand or by using a heavy-duty electric mixer, an automatic bread machine or a food processor.

- Mixing by hand takes about 10 minutes.
- The electric mixer takes about 5 minutes
- The food processor takes about 1 minute.
- Automated Bread Machines are programmed.

For a beginner, it is important to know how bread dough should feel during all stages of mixing. So try mixing by hand.

There are three methods to raise dough and create yeast breads. The first and the most traditional method involves mixing the yeast with a bit of sugar and a small amount of warm water and  allowing it to stand a few minutes until it activates, or proofs, which is known as the **Short** or **Direct method**. The proofed yeast is then mixed with the remaining ingredients to form dough.

Some recipes use the **Sponge method**, which involves making an initial batter with the yeast, some liquid and a small amount of flour to start fermentation. This batter is allowed to proof for an hour or up to a day before the remaining ingredients are added to form the bread dough. Any salt or fat listed in the recipe is added with the remaining flour when the dough is formed. The dough is mixed, raised, formed and baked as in any other bread recipe.

The final method is called the **Rapid Mix method**. It is a fast method of mixing dough, since proofing the yeast in liquid is not necessary. Yeast and a portion of dry ingredients are mixed with hot liquid (around 50 degrees Celsius), and then the remaining flour and the ingredients are added to form the dough.

Rising (fermentation)

Once the bread is mixed, it is then left to rise (ferment). As fermentation takes place, the dough slowly changes from a rough dense mass lacking extensibility and with poor gas holding properties, into a smooth, extensible dough with good gas holding properties. The yeast cells grow, the gluten protein pieces stick together to form networks, and alcohol and carbon dioxide are formed from the breakdown of carbohydrates (starch, sugars) that are found naturally in the flour.

The yeast uses sugars in much the same way as we do, i.e. it breaks sugar down into carbon dioxide and water. Enzymes present in yeast and flour also help to speed up this reaction. When there is plenty of oxygen present, the following reaction occurs. The energy, which is released, is used by the yeast for growth and activity. In bread dough, where the oxygen supply is limited, the yeast can only partially breakdown the sugar. Alcohol and carbon dioxide are produced in this process known as alcoholic fermentation. The carbon dioxide produced in these reactions causes the dough to rise (ferment or prove), and the alcohol produced mostly evaporates from the dough during the baking process.

During fermentation each yeast cell forms a centre around which carbon dioxide bubbles form. Thousands of tiny bubbles, each surrounded by a thin film of gluten, form cells inside the dough piece. The increase in dough size occurs as these cells fill with gas.

Kneading

Any large gas holes that may have formed during rising are released by kneading. Kneading is a logical and practical set of physical motions that transform dough from a rough, shaggy mass to a soft, pliable dough. Kneading strengthens the gluten fibres, and eventually creates a soft, firm honeycomb pattern in the cut slices of baked bread. It is always advisable to finish dough with some hand kneading, no matter how it has been mixed, to smoothen it out. The proteins in the wheat flour, called gluten, become stretchy when worked, creating a structure strong enough to contain the expanding carbon dioxide gas, the by-product of the yeast's reproduction.

Techniques of kneading are unique to each baker: some push, some press, some squeeze or slam. Some are gentle, others vigorous. There are hard kneaders and soft kneaders – your nature will determine which

Sticky

Push

Pull and turn

Tiny blisters

school you are from. Whatever the technique, if you are happy with the consistency of your dough and satisfied with the finished loaves, then you are doing a good job. Be certain that your work surface is at a height that allows easy movement of your arms at the elbows. Sprinkle a smooth marble, wood or plastic work surface with a light dusting of flour. This will prevent excessive sticking. If the dough sticks to the surface, it will inhibit the smooth, easy kneading motions. Scrape the shaggy dough mass out of the bowl with a spatula or a plastic dough scraper onto the floured work surface.

> It is always advisable to finish dough with some hand kneading, no matter how it has been mixed, to smoothen it out.

Whole wheat and rye dough tend to be denser, wetter and stickier than white dough. The amount of flour to be added will vary; the important thing is not to add too much.

Place one hand gently on the dough surface. With large, fluid movements, using the weight of your upper body, slowly push the dough away from your body with the heel of your hand. As you pull back, use the fingers to lift the farthest edge of the dough and fold it half back towards you and push away again. At the same time, you will be slowly turning the dough. The dough will slide across the surface, absorbing the small amount of flour it requires, going back and forth, turning slowly at the same time.

Repeat the sequence: push, turn and fold rhythmically. Use a pressure equal to the resistance felt. The dough will, at first, be quite soft, even sticky, needing gentle motions. The hand kneading process can take about 2-10 minutes, with hand-mixed dough taking more time and machine-mixed dough taking less.

If too much dough sticks to your hands, simply rub them together to flake off the excess. On the work surface, scrape up any large dry slabs of sticky dough and discard them. They will become dry patches in the dough. As you work, sprinkle additional flour only one tablespoon at a time on your work surface, this helps you maintain the maximum amount of control so that the dough will end up with the exact consistency you want.

As you learn from experience, the rhythm of your kneading motions will begin to adjust automatically to the tension in the dough. At this point the dough will lose its stickiness and evolve into a smooth ball with tiny blisters forming just under the skin. It will have two surfaces – a smooth one that is in contact with the work surface, and a creased, folded top. The smooth surface will absorb the flour while the top is being worked. If the dough is wet and slack, add more flour. But adding too much flour creates stiff dough and a dry baked loaf. This is by far the most common mistake made by the beginning bakers. Wholegrain and sweet dough should be softer than white dough, which are much stiffer, firmer and smoother. This is where experience eventually comes from.

Step 4

Dough Rising

Keep the kneaded dough in a narrow, deep container rather than in a wide shallow bowl. Deep plastic containers with lids for raising the dough serve the purpose best. Avoid wide metal bowls, which conduct heat easily and can 'cook' the dough if it rises in too warm a place. Grease the container by brushing with oil or melted butter and place the ball of dough in it, turning it once to grease the top to prevent drying and the formation of a crust. Plastic wrap is good as a cover, helping to retain the precious moisture and to inhibit the formation of a thick skin.

Note in mind or mark on the container where the dough will be when raised to double. It is difficult to predict the exact rising time, which depends on many factors, such as the temperature of the finished dough, the amount of yeast used and the general atmospheric conditions. Wholegrain breads and dough, high in fat and dry fruits content take longer than lean white-flour dough. That is why dry fruits or nuts are often added after the rising. Generally, a medium yeast dough will take 1½ to 2 hours to rise to the classic "double in bulk" stage at room temperature, about 23-25 degrees Celsius. Subsequent risings are about half as fast as the initial rise.

To slow down the rising of the dough, the dough can be placed in the refrigerator for 8 hours to overnight, covered tightly with plastic wrap to retain moisture. Dough that has been refrigerated must come back to room temperature to complete its rising process. So count on about 4 extra hours for the dough to return to room temperature.

Test to see if a dough has raised enough by poking 2 fingers into it. If the indentations remain, the dough is adequately raised. If not, recover the bowl and let the dough rest for 15 minutes longer before testing it again. If you are having trouble finding a good place to raise your dough or if you have a cold kitchen environment, you can consider some of the following choices:

- Turn on the oven to the lowest setting for 3 minutes.
- Turn off the heat and let the dough be in the oven with the door open for another 15-20 minutes.
- Place the bowl of dough in or over a pan of warm water.
- Rinse a large earthen bowl with warm water and invert it over the ball of dough.

Step 5

Deflating the dough

At this time, the dough will be light from lots of air and will be delicately dome-shaped. You can opt for hard deflating or gentle deflating dough. Smaller amounts of dough need gentle deflating, whereas larger amount need the fist action or punching down, done by pushing your fist into the centre of

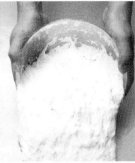

Punch to deflate

Deflate by turning out onto work surface

the dough and folding the edges towards the centre to expel the extra air. To deflate dough, turn it out onto a lightly-floured work surface. The act of turning out the dough will naturally deflate it. No more kneading is required at this time; it will reactivate the gluten and give the dough a springy tension that can make it difficult to shape up.

Step 6

Shaping a loaf and final rise

Divide the dough into equal portions. It is important that each portion be of the same size, so that each loaf rises and bakes in the small amount of time. Any embellishments like nuts or fruits can be added at this time by patting the dough into a large rectangle, sprinkling it with the ingredients as directed in the recipe, folding the dough into 1/3rd and kneading gently. This technique quickly distributes the nuts and fruits evenly in the dough.The shaping of dough is a highly individual technique and needs some practice. If the dough resists forming, cover it and let it rest for 10 minutes on the work surface to let it relax before continuing.

Use the right pan for baking bread. All bakers have their favourite pans, whether a precious heirloom or a disposable aluminium pan which requires no washing and minimum greasing. A pan, as stated in the subsequent recipes, is a guide

43

and not a law, but substitute a pan that has a similar dimension or volume for best results. No matter what size of pan is used, the formed dough should not fill more than two-thirds of the pan.

Filling the pan with less dough will give you flat dough; more produced and overflowing loaf that looks awkward and heavy on the top. When baking at high oven temperatures, stick two baking sheets together, a practice known as **"double panning"**, to slow down the temperature and to prevent the bottom of the baked goods from burning. Greasing a pan can make big difference, so note the specific instructions for each recipe. Since oil tends to be absorbed into the dough, use butter or margarine preferably. Oil works best with non-stick pan coatings. Pans can also be lined with the baking parchment paper or aluminium foil to prevent sticking and to facilitate the easier removal of the loaf.

Final rise. Once the loaf is formed, let the dough rise, with plastic wrap loosely draped over it at room temperature. The dough is ready when double in bulk or about 1 inch above the rim of the pan. However long it takes, give the dough enough time to fill the pans properly. When you put the dough in the pan, visualise what it would look like when it is of the right size to go into the oven. When it reaches that point, you will instantly recognise it.

The final rise *Risen and ready to bake*

Step 7

Glazing

Glazing may be applied before the loaf is placed in the oven or after it comes out of the oven. This is totally optional, depending upon the look you like your bread to have. An **egg glaze** produces a finished-looking shiny top surface coating that can also serve to adhere seeds or rolled oars to the crust. The yolk produces a crust and is often used in breads that are rich in fat and sugar. Beaten egg white makes a shiny light brown finish.

Milk and cream contribute to a dark, shiny finish and soften the crust. Melted butter and oils can be brushed on a loaf before, during or after baking to keep the crust soft and to add a better flavour. Sweet dough is usually drizzled with powdered sugar glaze as a flavour enhancer. Dusting with flour or with the combination of ground spices or flour gives an earthy matte finish. When applying a glaze, use a soft-bristled, clean pastry brush to apply, taking care not to puncture or deflate the loaf. Also take care not to allow the glaze to drip down into the sides of the pan, which would make the dough stick and not rise as high.

Step 8

Baking

First adjust the oven rack, and then preheat the oven for about 20 minutes. Then bake as directed in the recipe. Remember to lower the temperature of the oven by 5-10 degrees Celsius if using glass pans. The arrangement of the pans is very important. Place the pans in the preheated oven, on the centre or the lowest rack, unless the recipe states otherwise, for most even baking and well-browned crust, with at least 2 inches of space between the pans, never touching each other, and away from the oven wall for best heat circulation. Breads on baking sheets are best baked in the centre or lower third of the oven, one sheet at a time.

Baking time always depends on the size of the loaves as well as the temperature. After the first 10 minutes, you can open the oven door without affecting the finished shape. Check the bread at least 10 minutes earlier than the recipe specifies for complete baking, to look for signs of early or uneven browning. If the loaf is browning too quickly, tent it loosely with aluminium foil. If it is not brown enough, extend the baking time. If the bottom is still pale, remove the loaf from its pan, place the loaf directly on the rack, and bake it further for 8-10 minutes to brown. Round loaves always take longer to bake than long, thin ones.

Step 9

Cooling

When the bread is done, remove it immediately from the pans and cool completely on wire racks that allow the heat to dissipate from underneath before slicing. If you don't have a rack handy, cool the loaves on their sides across the edges of the baking pans or can use the fire tongs or any other raised wired platform to cool.

Bread has not finished baking until it is cool and the excess moisture from the inside of the loaf has evaporated. Bread should be cool before it is sliced; if you must cut warm bread, turn it on its sides to prevent squashing. Always use a sharp serrated knife for slicing so as not to tear the delicate crumb. Slice the loaves on a board with a sawing motion. Store sweet or cheese-filled loaves in the refrigerator and plain loaves at room temperature in a clean plastic bag or a bread box.

Step 10

Reheating and home freezing

Bread may be reheated in the oven at 175 degrees Celsius. Place the unsliced loaf in the preheated oven for 15-20 minutes to crisp the crust and heat through. Sliced breads and rolls reheat best when wrapped in aluminium foil.

Home freezing: Since homemade breads have no preservatives, you should freeze loaves that will not be eaten within 3 days. Home freezing is a simple and plain method of preserving food. The freezer compartment of a refrigerator is not a true deep-freeze but is intended for short storage. It will keep foods frozen for a few months, but for long-term safe storage, you should freeze at 'zero' degree or below.

To freeze yeast breads and dinner rolls, completely bake according to the recipe. Let cool to room temperature on a rack, which takes about 4 hours; otherwise the centre will freeze solid and defrost into a soggy mass. Wrap the loaves first in good quality plastic wrap, then enclose in aluminium foil or seal in a double layer of re-closable plastic freezer bags. The maximum storage time is about 3 months, but for the best flavour and texture, store no longer than 1 month. To thaw, let the loaf stand at room temperature for about 3 hours, completely wrapped to preserve the moisture, shaking out any accumulation of ice crystals. Unwrap and reheat at the temperature at which the bread was baked, for about 8-10 minutes.

Since homemade breads have no preservatives, you should freeze loaves that will not be eaten within 3 days.

Weights

- 1 ounce (oz.) = 28 gm (30 gm, rounding off to multiple of 5 gm for ease)
- 1 pound flour = 4 cups
- 2.2 pounds = 1 kg

Measures

- 1 fluid ounce (fl. oz) = 30 ml
- An average teacup is about 210 ml (7 fl. oz)
- 1 teaspoon = 5 ml
- 1 tablespoon = 15 ml

Temperatures

- 360° F (Fahrenheit) = 182° C (Celsius)
- While baking in a glass pan the temperature should be lowered by 50° F (10° C), as glass absorbs heat quickly.
- Following is the formula that can be used for temperature conversions. $(F - 32)/9 = C/5$

State of the Oven	Fahrenheit (F)	Celcius (C)
SLOW	250-300	120-150
MODERATE	325-375	165-190
HOT	400-450	205-230
VERY HOT	475-500	245-260

Dough won't rise

- If forgotten to add the yeast
- If yeast was inactive or it was killed with liquid that was too hot
- Due to low gluten content in flour or too high a percentage of wholegrain flour or using of old flour and finally if you are using too much flour
- If the ingredients were cold, so the dough made with them was cold
- If the dough was raised in too cool area, where it takes two to three times the usual amount of time to rise

❖ ❖ ❖

Texture is coarse

- Too much liquid in proportion to the flour
- Risen too long before baking
- Oven temperature is too low during baking

❖ ❖ ❖

Flat top crust

- Risen too long in the pan causing it to collapse in the pan
- Opening the oven door during the first ten minutes of baking before the crumb is set

49

Trouble shooters

Texture crumbly and dry

- Too long a rise at too high a temperature

❖ ❖ ❖

Flat, small loaf

- Too much salt
- Dough was undermixed
- Not enough flour, leaving the dough too soft to hold its own shape
- Dough overfermented in pan and then collapsed in the oven
- Pan too large for dough
- Oven temperature too hot during baking

❖ ❖ ❖

One side higher than the other

- Uneven oven heat; next time rotate pans halfway through baking

❖ ❖ ❖

Shelling (top crust separates)

- Overmixing
- Top dried out during rising
- Oven temperature too low
- Too much yeast in the recipe

❖ ❖ ❖

Bread rose over pan sides

- Pan too small for the dough
- Not enough salt to control yeast activity
- Overrisen in the pans
- Oven temperature too low

❖ ❖ ❖

Dark crust

- Oven temperature too high

❖ ❖ ❖

Pale crust

- Not baked long enough; remove from the pan and bake 5-10 minutes longer directly on oven rack
- Oven temperature too low during baking
- Pans set too close together in the oven

❖ ❖ ❖

Streaky interior look

- Improper mixing of the dough
- Dough dried out during rising

❖ ❖ ❖

Porous texture and strong yeast odour

- Too much yeast used in proportion to the flour

❖ ❖ ❖

Yeasty taste

- Too long a rise at too high a temperature
- Too much yeast
- Underbaked

❖ ❖ ❖

Chewy and dry texture

- Too little fat in proportion to the other ingredients

❖ ❖ ❖

Thick and tough crust

- Too much flour
- Oven temperature too low during baking

batter bread

A perfect recipe to start for the first-time bread bakers is batter bread. This requires no kneading; the process is not only quicker than for regular bread dough but also tidier, with less clean up. If you don't have enough time to prepare kneaded bread, this type of loaf is perfect – it rises at once and then bakes.

Batter breads are yeast-risen loaves that are not kneaded but beaten vigorously with a wooden spoon or an electric mixer, for soft, sticky dough. The beating develops the gluten in the dough in a manner similar to kneading and gives the batter a moist consistency.

You will note that an exact amount of flour is called for in the ingredient list, rather than an approximate amount, like regular yeast dough. This is because a very specific texture is what you are going for. This batter also calls for a pinch of ground ginger, an old-fashioned tradition that stimulates the activity of the yeast because the dough is quite delicate; it can collapse in the oven if allowed to rise too long, no matter what type of baking mould you use.

The rising time for batter breads is crucial to their success, so care needs to be taken here.

Batter breads can be baked in many types of moulds – coffee cans, oven proof glass baking canisters, mini stoneware bread crocks, and regular loaf and tube pans of any size. Just remember to fill only one-half to two-thirds full.

If your baking dish is too small, make a sturdy collar out of foil, extending the sides up and fastening the collar with kitchen twine around the can. This will enclose the rising dough during baking and produce a beautiful domed loaf.

Batter breads are best eaten the day they are baked, and they taste great when toasted. Because of their round shape, they are quite preferred as the base for poached eggs.

White Velvet Batter Bread

This is a unique no-knead loaf that fills the kitchen with an incredible aroma, while it bakes. Since it takes only one rise in the moulds, it takes about two hours from mixing to the table. It utilises creamy evaporated milk, which has about 60% of its water removed and gives the bread an especially delicate, moist texture. Most bakers prefer to bake it in coffee cans, creating the special mushroom shape. In case coffee cans are not available, glass-baking canisters can be used.

To make two loaves, you require:
Bakeware: Two 400 ml glass-baking canisters

Ingredients

- 1 tablespoon (15 gm) active dry yeast
- 3 tablespoons light brown sugar
- ¼ tablespoon brown ginger
- ½ cup warm water (40-45 degrees Celsius)
- 1 can (360 ml) evaporated milk at room temperature
- 2 teaspoons (10 gm) salt
- 2 tablespoons walnut oil or unsalted butter, melted
- 4¼ cups all-purpose flour

Method

Follow the steps given below carefully.

Step 1 – Mixing the batter

In a small bowl, sprinkle the yeast, a pinch of brown sugar and the ginger over the warm water. Stir till the mixture gets dissolved and let stand until foamy for about 10 minutes.

Batter can be made by hand and also by a mixer.

Mixing by hand

Combine the milk, remaining sugar, salt, oil or butter, and 1½ cups of flour in a large bowl. Beat vigorously with a balloon whisk or a dough whisk, applying at least about 40-50 strokes by hand, till thick and sticky. Add the yeast mixture and beat vigorously for about 1 minute more. Gradually add the remaining flour, ½ cup at a time, beat vigorously another 100 strokes for about two minutes. The batter will stay sticky. Scrape down the sides of the bowl with a spatula.

By a mixer

Combine the milk, remaining sugar, salt, oil or butter, and 1½ cups of the flour in the bowl of the heavy-duty electric mixer fitted with a paddle attachment. Beat for 1 minute on medium speed, or until thick and sticky. Add the yeast mixture and beat for 1 minute more. Continue to add the remaining flour on low speed, ½ cup at a time, then beat vigorously for about 2 minutes on medium speed. The batter will stay sticky. Scrape down the sides with a spatula.

Step 2 – Panning and Rising

Grease the bottom and the sides of the container (coffee can or the canisters) generously with oil. Divide the batter evenly between the two moulds, filling ½ to 2/3ʳᵈ full. Use a spatula to push the batter into the corners and smooth the top with flour-dusted fingers. Cover loosely with plastic wrap, lightly greased with vegetable oil and let rise at room temperature until double in bulk. In about 45 minutes to 1 hour, the batter should be levelled with the rim of the pan.

Slightly lift up the plastic wrap. Do not let the dough rise more than the double (over-risen loaves collapse during baking). If the batter over-rises, beat vigorously about 20 strokes, then return it to the pan and begin the rising again.

About 20 minutes before baking, place the oven rack in the lower part of the oven and pre-heat the oven to 175 degrees Celsius.

Bake for 40-45 minutes, until the top is crusty and dark brown. The bread should sound hollow when tapped. Put a knife in the centre of the baked loaf to test whether it has baked from the inside or not. The crown of the loaves will dome about 3-4 inches above the rim of the mould. Cool in the moulds for about 5 minutes. Turn the moulds on its side and slide the loaves out onto a cooling rack to cool for at least 2 hours. Serve slightly warm, sliced into thick rounds or cut into long wedges, laced with butter.

You can also store them, wrapped in plastic food storage bags at room temperature for about three days or in the freezer for upto 2 months.

Other Batter Breads

Depending upon the flavour and taste, you can make your own batter breads. Remember the preparation method remains the same except the ingredients. You can try the recipes given below and relish the taste.

Cranberry and Raisin nut batter bread

Ingredients

- 1 teaspoon ground Cinnamon
- ½ teaspoon ground Nutmeg
- 1/3 cup golden Raisins
- 1/3 cup dried Cranberries and
- 3 tablespoons chopped Walnuts

Mix the above ingredients into the batter during the mixing after adding the sugar.

Preparation method remains the same.

Light wheat batter bread

- Substitute 1½ cups wholewheat flour for 1-½ cups of the all-purpose flour.
- Substitute ¼ cup honey for the brown sugar.

Add everything to the batter during the mixing. Preparation method remains the same.

Orange Rye batter bread

- Substitute 1½ cups medium Rye flour for 1 cup of the all-purpose flour.
- Substitute light molasses for the brown sugar.
- 1 grated zest of orange.
- 2 tablespoons thawed frozen orange juice.
- 1½ teaspoons caraway seeds (Shahi Jeera).

Mix all the above ingredients to the batter during the mixing after adding the sugar. Preparation method remains the same.

White batter bread with fennel

- Substitute olive oil for the walnut oil or butter.
- 1 tablespoon fennel seeds.

Mix everything to the batter during the mixing after adding the sugar. Preparation method remains the same.

Oatmeal-prune batter bread

Substitute ½ cup rolled oats for ½ cup of the all-purpose flour. Fold 1½ cups snipped, moist pitted prunes (dried plum) into the batter after the mixing and adding the sugar. Preparation method remains the same.

Cornmeal-herb batter bread

Substitute ½ cup medium yellow cornmeal for ½ cup of the all-purpose flour. Add ½ teaspoon dried tarragon leaves; ½ teaspoon dried summer savoury leaves, and dried thyme leaves to the batter during the mixing and after adding the sugar. Preparation method remains the same.

an egg bread

In the busy schedule, we hurry up making easy recipes like omelettes or boiled eggs for breakfast. Eggs can be used in varieties of recipes, even in bread. Eggs not only contribute to the characteristic colour and flavour to the bread but also add to its nutritional value.

Egg bread has centuries of historical and symbolic significance. Egg bread, also known as *Challah*, fills the description of manna in the Bible, a lovely home-baked whitish loaf dotted with dark seeds. It was the mainstay of the abundant Jewish celebration table, where the word 'Bread' means food. Egg breads are so satisfying to master (and eat!) that many bakers never make anything else.

The eggs add a wonderful pale yellow colour to the interior, a colour so treasured that saffron was used to imitate the colour in the event the requisite eggs were not available. Eggs also add a rich flavour and a tender, cake like texture to breads; qualities that no other ingredients can produce.

Customary shapes include simple three-strand and intricate six-strand breads, spiral rounds, ovals, ladders, triangles, tiny pan loaves and baby knots. Crowns are filled with anything from raisins and nuts, to poppy seeds and chocolate. Many of the shapes have some relevance to Jewish traditions.

Eggs are considered as a liquid measure ingredient. Modern recipes are designed for the use of one to six large eggs; the master recipe here uses four. As a guide, three small eggs may be substituted for two large eggs in recipes. One large egg equals ¼th cup liquid measure. While of a large egg equals three tablespoons and the yolk equals one tablespoon.

Classic Challah Egg Bread

Before trying any kneaded dough, it is recommended to try and bake egg bread. It is easy to handle and the egg gives the extra leavening power that effortlessly compensates for any irregularities in the rising or forming of the dough. The end result is fluffy, tender bread. The egg bread is in great demand at special gatherings and during holidays.

**To make three standard loaves or two, you require:
Bakeware: three 9×5-inch loaf pans or two 11×17-inch
baking sheets.**

Ingredients

- 2 cups warm water (40 to 45 degrees Celsius)
- 1½ tablespoons Active Dry Yeast
- Pinch of sugar
- 8 to 8¼ cups All-purpose or Bread flour
- 1 tablespoon Salt
- 4 large Eggs
- ½ cup Honey, slightly warm for easy pouring
- 2/3 cup vegetable or light Olive oil
- 1 large egg beaten with one tablespoon water for glaze
- 2 tablespoons sesame seeds or Poppy seeds for sprinkling (optional)

Method

Follow the steps given below carefully.

Step 1 – Mixing the Dough

Pour half cup of the warm water into a small bowl. Sprinkle the yeast and sugar over the surface. Stir to dissolve and let stand at room temperature until foamy, for about 10 minutes. The batter can be made by hand and also by mixer.

To make by hand

Place 1½ cups of the flour and the salt in a large bowl. Make a hole in the centre of the flour and add the eggs, honey, and oil and remaining 1½ cups of water. Using a balloon or dough whisk beat vigorously for about 1 minute. Add the yeast mixture and beat vigorously for 1 minute more, or until the dough comes together. Switch to a wooden spoon when the dough clogs the whisk. Add the remaining flour, ½ cup at a time, until soft, shaggy dough, that just pulls away from the sides of the bowl, is formed.

If using a heavy-duty electric mixer fitted with the paddle attachment, place 1½ cups of the flour and the salt in the work bowl. Add the eggs, honey, oil and the remaining 1½ cups water on low speed. When combined, beat until smooth on medium-low speed, about 1 minute. Add the yeast mixture and beat on medium speed for 1 minute more. Switch to low speed and add the remaining flour, 1/3 cup at a time, until soft, shaggy dough that just clears the sides of the bowl is formed. Switch to the dough hook when the dough thickens, about two-thirds through adding the flour, and knead for about 4 minutes on medium speed until the dough works its way up the hook. The dough will make a soft ball and pull away from the sides of the bowl. Pull it out and finish kneading by hand.

Step 2 – Kneading

Turn the dough out onto a lightly floured work surface. Knead until firm yet still springy, 1 minute for a machine mixed dough and 5-7 minutes for a hand-mixed dough, dusting with flour, 1 tablespoon at a time, just enough to prevent the dough from sticking to your hand and the work surface. The dough will be very smooth, have a soft elastic quality, not stiff and will hold its shape.

Step 3 – Rising

Place the dough ball in a greased deep container, turn once to grease the top and cover loosely with a plastic wrap. If using a mixer, you can put on the cover to let the dough rise in the bowl.

Mark the container to indicate how high the dough will be when raised to double. Let it rise at room temperature until double in bulk, for about 2-2½ hours. Do not allow the dough to rise more than double; over-risen dough have a tendency to tear, and the baked loaf will not be as fluffy as it should be.

Gently deflate the dough by inserting your fist in its centre, re-cover and let rise again until double in bulk, for about 1-1½ hours. This second rise can be skipped, but the flavour is much nicer if you can give the dough the extra time.

Step 4 – Shaping the Dough and the Final Rise

Turn the dough out onto a lightly floured work surface; it will deflate. Lightly grease the bottom and sides of the 3 loaf pans or line the 2 baking sheets with parchment paper to prevent sticking. Divide the dough according to the bakeware used. Further divide each portion into 3 equal portions.

Using your palms, roll each section into a fat cylinder about 10 inches long for the pan loaf, and about 16 inches long for the free-form dough, which are tapered at each end. Be sure that these ropes are of equal size and shape.

Place 3 ropes parallel to each other. Begin braiding, starting in the centre rather than at the ends for a more even shape. Adjust or press the bread to make it look even. Tuck the ends under and set into the loaf pan or on the baking sheet, pinching the ends into the tapered points.

Beat the egg and the water glaze with a fork until foamy. Using a pastry brush, brush the tops of the loaf with some of the egg mixture. Do not let the egg glaze drip down into the

sides of the pan or it will make the breads stick and inhibit the rising in the oven.

Cover the loaves loosely with plastic wrap and let rise at room temperature until the dough is almost double in bulk and about 1 inch over the rims of the pans, for about 45 minutes. Do not let this dough rise longer before baking.

Step 5 – Baking, Cooling and Storage

Place the oven rack in the middle of the oven and pre-heat the oven to 175 degrees Celsius (160 degrees Celcius if using glass pans). Brush the surface a second time with the egg glaze and  sprinkle with the seeds, if desired.

Bake for 40-45 minutes, or until the loaves are deep golden brown, the sides have slightly shrunk away from the pan. And the bread sounds hollow when tapped on the top or bottom with your finger. Remove the pans and transfer to a cooling rack. Let it cool to room temperature before slicing. Store the breads wrapped in a plastic food storage bag at room temperature for up to 3 days or in the freezer for 2 months.

Wheat and Honey Challah Egg Bread

The wheat and honey challah egg bread is certainly not traditional, but many modern bakers prefer it for its flavour. It will still be lovely, light-textured bread. To its ingredients, substitute 3½ cups wholewheat flour for an equal amount of all-purpose flour. Other things remain the same. Even mix, rise, shape, glaze and bake as like Classic Challah Egg Bread.

Challah Cinnamon Swirl

Cinnamon bread is probably the simplest and the most popular American sweet bread a home baker can bake. It can be fashioned from any number of bread doughs that vary in richness or in type of grains used and the amount of cinnamon in the filling can also be varied. Use a really good grade of ground cinnamon for a distinctive flavour. Be sure that the dough does not over-rise in the pans; otherwise there will be a gap between the filling and the bread.

To make three loaves, you require:
Bakeware: Three 9×5-inch loaf pans.

Ingredients

- 1 cup Sugar
- ¼ cup ground Cinnamon
- 1 recipe Classic Challah Egg Bread dough
- Milk for brushing
- 1 large egg beaten with 1 tablespoon milk, for glaze

Method

Follow the steps given below carefully.

Lightly grease the bottom and the sides of the loaf pans. Mix the Sugar and Cinnamon together in a small bowl.

Prepare the dough through the end of step 3. (page 61)

To shape the loaves, turn the risen dough out onto the work surface and divide into thirds. Pat each portion into a 9×14 inch rectangle and brush with the milk. Sprinkle evenly with 1/3 of the Cinnamon-sugar, leaving a ½ inch border all the way round. Starting at the long edge, roll up in jellyroll fashion into a tight log. Pinch the bottom seam closed, then

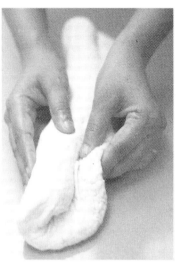

pull up the ends and also pinch to seal. This is to prevent the filling from leaking out. Repeat the filling and shaping with the other two portions. Place the loaves, seam side down, in the pans. Cover loosely with plastic wrap and let rise at room temperature until almost double in bulk and about 1 inch above the rims of the pans, 1-1½ hours.

When the dough has risen to just above the rims of the pans, adjust the oven racks to the lower third position and pre-heat the oven to 175 degrees Celsius (160 degrees Celcius if using glass).

Beat the egg and the milk with a fork until foamy. Using a pastry brush, gently brush the tops of the loaves with some of the egg glaze. Bake for 30-40 minutes, or until the loaves are deep golden brown, the sides have slightly shrunk away from the pan, and the bread sounds hollow when tapped on the top or the bottom with your fingers. Remove the loaves from the pan and transfer to a cooling rack. Let cool to room temperature before slicing.

Rum Raisin – Cinnamon Breakfast Sweet Rolls

Cinnamon rolls are everyone's favourite. They are easy to make and are incredibly delicious. The rum raisins burst in your mouth and make these rolls pure breakfast pleasure. Serve warm with butter.

To make 16 large rolls, you require:
Bakeware: One 11×17-inch baking sheet or large roasting pan.

Ingredients

- ¼ recipe Classic Challah Egg Bread dough

For Filling

- 1 cup dark Raisins
- 1/3 dark Rum (dark-coloured Rum)
- 1 cup firmly packed light Brown Sugar
- 4 teaspoons ground Cinnamon
- 3 tablespoons unsalted butter, melted

For Roll Icing

- 2 cups sifted powdered Sugar
- 3½ tablespoons Milk
- 1 teaspoon Vanilla extract

Method

Line the baking sheet with parchment. Prepare the dough through the end of step 3 (Given in page 61).

To make the filling, combine the raisins with the Rum in a small bowl and toss to coat evenly. Cover and let rest for 30 minutes to plump. Combine the Brown Sugar and Cinnamon in a small bowl.

To shape the dough, turn the risen dough out onto a lightly floured work surface. Roll or pat into a 12×16 inch rectangle. Leaving a ½-inch border all around the edges of the rectangle, brush the surface heavily with the melted butter, then sprinkle evenly with the Brown Sugar filling.

Drain the Raisins, reserving the Rum for another purpose, and sprinkle the dough with the Raisins.

Starting from the long edge, roll up in jellyroll fashion and pinch the bottom seam to seal; leave the ends open with the fillings exposed.

Using a gentle sawing motion with a serrated knife, cut the roll into 16 equal 1-inch portions. The easiest way to do this is to mark the halfway point first, and divide the roll in half, then divide the halves again in halves, and then divide each quarter into 4 equal slices.

As a guide, three small eggs may be substituted for two large eggs in recipes. One large egg equals ¼th cup liquid measure. White of a large egg equals three tablespoons and the yolk equals one tablespoon.

Place the slices, cut side down, 1 inch apart on the baking sheet. (I make 4 rows of four across). Cover loosely with plastic wrap and let the rolls rise at room temperature until puffy and double, about 45 minutes. The rolls will touch each other when raised.

Adjust the oven rack to the centre position and pre-heat the oven to 175 degrees Celsius for 20 minutes.

Bake the rolls in the centre of the oven until the tops are golden brown for 20-25 minutes. Remove from the oven, place the pan on the wire rack and let the pan cool for 15 minutes.

Meanwhile, make the icing: combine the sugar, milk and vanilla in a small bowl. Using a wire whisk beat vigorously until smooth. Using a large spoon, drizzle each roll with icing. Let stand until cool to set the glaze.

Onion Pretzel

These little breads, which resemble focaccia are also known as onion boards. Cut into portions to serve with cheese, or split horizontally for sandwiches.

To make 4 flat breads, you require:
Bakeware: Four 9-inch round or 8-inch square pans.

Ingredients

- ½ recipe Classic Challah Egg Bread dough
- ¼ cup Olive oil
- 2 medium Onions, diced
- 1½ tablespoons Poppy seeds
- Coarse sea salt

Method

Grease the pans with some of the Olive oil. Prepare the dough through the end of step 3 (Given in page 61).

To shape, turn the risen dough out onto the work surface and divide it into 4 equal portions. Roll out with a rolling pin about 1 ¼ inch thick to fit the pans. Brush each portion with Olive oil, sprinkle with Onions, leaving a 1-inch border all the way around, and press in slightly. Sprinkle with Poppy seeds and coarse Salt. Let stand at room temperature for 15 minutes, uncovered.

Pre-heat the oven to 190 degrees Celsius (175 degrees Celcius if using glass pans) for 20 minutes. Place the oven rack in the centre position and bake for 25-30 minutes, or until the edges are browned and the Onion soft.

Loosen the Onion boards with a metal spatula and slide out of the pans onto a wire rack to cool completely before serving.

The Best Hamburger Buns

The easiest way to eat a burger is on a soft bun, nothing so thick that it won't fit in the mouth or too chewy. These buns keep well in the freezer, ready to be defrosted and cut in half.

You can vary the toppings with anything from black Pepper to black Sesame or Fennel seeds to the more conventional sesame or Poppy seeds.

To make 12 Buns, you require:
Bakeware: One 11×17-inch baking sheet.

Ingredients

- ½ recipe Classic Challah Egg Bread dough
- 1 large Egg beaten with 1 tablespoon water, for glaze
- 3 tablespoons Sesame seeds or Poppy seeds for sprinkling (optional)

Method

Line the baking sheet with parchment paper. Prepare the dough through the end of step 3 (Given in page 61).

To shape the buns, turn the risen dough out onto the work surface and divide in half. Divide each half into six equal portions. Form each portion into a ball by rolling the dough with cupped hands until smooth, smooth side up, on the baking sheet at least 2 inches apart.

Bake burns in the centre of the oven until golden brown and firm to touch, 18-22 minutes. Buns keep well in the freezer, ready to be defrosted and cut in half. You can vary the toppings with anything from black Pepper to black Sesame to the more conventional sesame or Poppy seeds.

Flatten each ball into a 1-inch high disc, about 3 inches in diameter, with your palm. Cover loosely with plastic wrap and let rise at room temperature until puffy, in about 30 minutes. Half way through the rising time, gently press to flatten a bit more.

Adjust the oven rack to the centre position and pre-heat the oven to 175 degrees Celsius for 20 minutes.

Brush the rolls with egg glaze; leave plain or sprinkle with Seeds. Bake in the centre of the oven until golden brown and firm to touch, 18-22 minutes. Transfer to a cooling rack to cool, and cut each bun horizontally in two halves.

Challah Dinner Knots

This egg-rich dough is perfect for baking the soft, delectable dinner roll.

To make 36 Dinner Rolls, you require:
Bakeware: Two 11×17-inch baking sheets.

Ingredients

- 1 recipe Classic Challah Egg Bread dough with the Honey reduced to 2 tablespoons.
- 1 large egg beaten with 1 tablespoon Milk for glaze
- 2 tablespoons Sesame or Poppy seeds for sprinkling

Method

Line the baking sheets with parchment paper. Prepare the dough through the end of step 3 (Given in page 61).

To shape the knots, turn the risen dough onto the work surface and divide in half. Divide each half into 18 equal portions. Roll each portion into a rope about 7 inches long and 1 inch wide. Cross one side over the other about 1 inch from the ends to form a large loop.

Take the tip of the piece that is on the top and carefully tuck it under and then through the centre hole to tie loosely into a knot. The end should pop up through and fill the loophole.

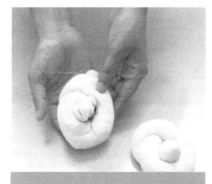

Tuck the other end under. Arrange the twisted knots 2 inches apart on the baking sheet (3 rolls of 6 knots). Cover loosely with plastic wrap and let rise until nearly doubled, about 20 minutes.

Meanwhile adjust the oven rack to the centre position and pre-heat the oven to 190 degrees Celsius for 20 minutes.

Brush the knots with egg glaze and

To shape the knots, take the tip of the piece that is on the top and carefully tuck it under and then through the centre hole to tie loosely into a knot. The end should pop up through and fill the loophole.

sprinkle with sesame or poppy seeds. Bake for 15-20 minutes, or until golden brown. Cool on baking sheets. Serve warm or at room temperature.

You can freeze them up to 2 months in the freezer.

a white bread

Plain white bread is the experienced baker's domain and new territory for the beginner to explore – beautiful, rich white bread with a faint trace of sweetness and a moist, even texture.

It is a mystery, how white bread got such a bad reputation. Most commercial loaves end up being spongy textured bread with no flavour, and this is what many people have come to think of when they are offered white bread. This, after all, is the loaf that made toast famous.

Homemade white bread is delicious and nutritious as well. Since most flours are enriched with minerals and vitamins, white breads are almost as good for us as wholewheat breads, just minus the fibre.

Breads made with the finest white wheat flour have historically been the most coveted of foods. They are still one of the most popular breads made, either at home or commercially.

Until the high-powered grain mills of the 19th century were able to separate the bran from the ground starchy endosperm, refined white wheat flour was expensive and scarce; dark breads made from coarsely ground wholegrains were the norm.

Modern bakers are able to choose from a large selection of finely ground white wheat flours, both all-purpose and bread flours, from which to make homemade loaves of premium quality and flavour.

Many white bread formulas incorporate milk or buttermilk, eggs, sugar and some fat, to make a memorable tasting loaf. Since the flour is still the predominant ingredient, its quality will dramatically affect how your loaf will look and taste.

Don't pass up the opportunity to buy stone-ground white flour if you ever visit a small mill; the flavour and texture will have you craving more.

Plain white bread is the basis for adding other ingredients that will accentuate its flavour: maple syrup, honey or sugar; grated citrus zest, herbs or spices; seeds and nuts; cheese and eggs. The loaves can be glazed or drizzled with a powdered sugar icing, or shaped into twists and breads. The loaves can be made in a variety of sizes; from sandwich-size loaves to individual mini loaves, which always delight since each person can cut into his/her own loaf.

One recipe made with about 6 cups of flour, baked at 190 degrees Celsius will make the following:

- Two 9×5×3 inch loaves with a baking time of 40-45 minutes
- Two 8½×4½×2½-inch loaves with a baking time of 35-40 minutes
- Four 7½×4×2-inch loaves with a baking time of 30-35 minutes
- Eight 6×3×2-inch loaves with a baking time of 25-30 minutes
- Sixteen 4×2½×2-inch individual loaves with a baking time of 18-24 minutes

Milk Bread

To make 2 loaves, you require:
Bakeware: Two 9×5-inch metal, non-stick aluminium, glass, or clay loaf pans

Ingredients

- 6-6½ unbleached All-purpose or Bread flour
- 2 tablespoons granulated Sugar
- 1 scant tablespoon (1 package) Active dry yeast
- 2 teaspoons Salt
- 2 cups warm Milk (about 35-40 degrees Celcius)
- ¼ cup boiling Water
- 3 tablespoons Soya, light Olive, or Vegetable oil
- 1 egg mixed with 1 tablespoon Milk, for glaze

Method

Follow the steps given below carefully.

Step 1 – Mixing the Dough

Assemble the ingredients and the equipment around your work surface. Set your mixing bowl, measuring cups and spoons, dough scrapper and whisk, and wooden spoon or heavy-duty mixer in the centre of the work surface. Place the flour container to the side for easy access during kneading. You can make batter by hand and also by mixer.

To make by hand

Combine two cups of flour, the sugar, yeast and salt in a large bowl. Combine the milk, boiling water and oil in a small bowl. The mixture should read somewhere between 40 and 50 degrees Celsius on a thermometer. It should feel hot to touch. Make a well in the centre of the dry ingredients and pour in the liquid mixture. Using a balloon or a dough whisk beat for about 3 minutes, scraping the bowl occasionally. Add ½ cup of flour and beat vigorously for 3 minutes longer. Switch to a wooden spoon when the dough clogs the whisk. Add the remaining flour, ½ cup at a time, beating for three minutes more to make stiff, shaggy dough that just clears the sides of the bowl.

To make by mixer

If using a heavy-duty electric mixer fitted with the paddle attachment, combine 2 cups of flour, the sugar, yeast and the

Siff and shaggy dough

Smooth & satiny after kneading

salt in the work bowl. Combine the milk, boiling water and oil in a small bowl. The mixture should read at 45 degrees Celsius. It should feel hot to touch. On low speed, pour the liquid ingredients into the dry ingredients. Increase the speed to medium-low and beat for two minutes. Add ½ cup of flour and beat vigorously 2 minutes more. Switch to low speed, and add the remaining flour, ½ cup at a time, until soft dough, that clears the sides of the bowl, is formed, 2 minutes more. Switch to the dough hook when the dough thickens, and knead for 2 minutes on medium speed, or until the dough works its way up the hook. The dough will make a soft ball, pull away from the sides of the bowl and roll around.

Step 2 – Kneading

Using a plastic dough card, turn the dough out onto a lightly floured work surface. Knead until firm yet smooth and satiny, less than 1 minute for a machine-mixed dough and 5-8 minutes for a hand-mixed dough, dusting with flour only 1 tablespoon at a time, as needed to prevent the dough from sticking to your hands and the work surface.

Step 3 – Rising

Place the dough ball in a greased deep container, turn once to grease the top, and cover with a plastic wrap. If using a mixer, you can put on the cover to let the dough rise on the bowl. Mark the container to indicate how high the dough will be when risen.

Let rise at room temperature until double in bulk, 1½-2 hours. Do not allow the dough to rise over double. To test the dough, press a fingertip into the top to see if the indentation remains. If the indentation fills back in quickly, the dough needs to rise more. Do not worry or rush the dough if it takes longer.

Step 4 – Shaping the Dough and the Final Rise

Lightly grease the bottom and the side of two 9×5-inch loaf pans. Turn the dough out on a clean work surface; it will naturally deflate. Using a metal bench scraper or a knife, divide  the dough into 4 equal portions without tearing the dough. With the palms of your hand, roll onto 4 flat oblong sausages, each about 10 inches long. Place 2 of the pieces side by side.

Holding both the pieces together at one end, wrap one around the other 2 or 3 times to create a flat twist effect. Place in the pans and tuck under the ends. Repeat to form the second loaf. Cover loosely with plastic wrap and let rise at room temperature until the dough is almost double in bulk, about one inch over the rims of the pan, about one hour.

Step 5 – Baking, Cooling and Storage

Place the oven rack in the middle of the oven and preheat the oven to 190 degrees Celsius (175 degrees Celsius, if using glass) for about 20 minutes.

Using a pastry brush, brush the tops of the loaves with the egg glaze. Do not let the egg glaze drip down into the sides of the pan or the bread will stick. Bake for 40-45 minutes or until the loaves are deep golden brown, the sides have slightly shrunk away from the pan, and the bread sounds hollow when tapped on the top with your finger. Lift one end of the loaf up out of the pan to peek underneath to check for an even browning on the bottom.

Immediately remove the loaves from the pans and set them on a cooling rack to cool. For proper cooling, air must circulate all around the loaf, so leave plenty of room between the loaves to keep the crust from getting soggy. After 15-20 minutes slice the loaves with a sharp knife.

Milk bread stays moist for about 3 days. You can store the unsliced bread, wrapped in a plastic food storage bag, at room temperature or in the freezer up to 2 months.

Cornmeal Honey Bread

Substitute one-cup yellow cornmeal flour for an equal amount of flour. Substitute an equal amount of honey for the sugar. The preparation method is same as for Milk Bread.

Caraway Light Rye Bread

Substitute 1½ cups Rye flour for an equal amount of All-purpose or Bread flour. Substitute an equal amount of molasses for the sugar and add 1 tablespoon Caraway seeds to the dough during the mixing after adding the sugar. The preparation method is same as for Milk Bread.

Raisin Bread

As the name implies, this bread calls for a large amount of raisins. The raisins are added after the rising of the dough where they are sprinkled over the dough. The dough is then gently kneaded so as to distribute them and is shaped in the form of loaf. You can top the loaves with sesame seeds or coarse granulated sugar.

To make two loaves, you require:
Bakeware: Two 9×5-inch loaf pans

Ingredients

- 1 recipe Milk Bread dough
- 1½ cups Golden Raisin
- 1½ cups Dark Raisins
- 1 egg mixed with 1-tablespoon Milk, for glaze
- 3 tablespoons Sesame seeds or coarse granulated sugar, for sprinkling

Method

Lightly grease the bottom and the sides of the two loaf pans. Prepare the dough through the end of step 3 (Given in page 76).

To shape the loaves, turn the risen dough out onto the work surface and divide it in half. Pat each portion into a 9×12-inch rectangle and sprinkle with ¾ cup each of the golden and dark raisins. Press in gently with your palms, then knead to distribute evenly. Pat each portion into a rectangle, roughly 8×6 inches in size. Fold the two short ends in 1 inch towards the middle. Starting at the long edge, roll up in jellyroll fashion into a tight log to form a standard loaf shape. Pinch the seam and the ends to seal.

When placing the loaf into the pan, tuck the ends under to make a neat, snug fit. The log should be of even thickness and fill the pan about 2/3 full. Cover loosely with plastic wrap. Repeat with the second portion and remaining raisins. Let rise at room temperature until the dough is fully double in bulk and about 1 inch over the rims of the pan, about 45 minutes.

Place the oven rack to the lower third position and pre-heat the oven to 190 degrees Celsius (175 degrees Celsius if using glass), for about 20 minutes.

Brush the loaves with the egg glaze and sprinkle with sesame seeds or sugar. Bake for 40-45 minutes, or until the loaves are browned and the bottoms sound hollow when tapped with your finger. Remove the loaves from the pans and transfer to a cooling rack to cool completely.

Cheese Mini Loaves

To make 16 loaves, you require:
Bakeware: Sixteen 4×2½×2-inch loaf pans

Ingredients

- 1 recipe Milk Bread dough
- 2 cups Grated Cheddar Cheese
- 1 egg mixed with 1 tablespoon Milk for glaze

Method

Lightly grease the bottom and sides of the 16 loaf pans.

Prepare the dough, adding the liquid mixture to the dry ingredients and beat for three minutes. Add ½ cup of flour, beat well, and then add the cheese. Continue mixing, kneading, and rising. To shape the dough, turn the risen dough out onto the work surface and divide it into 16 equal portions. Pat each portion into a 4×6-inch rectangle. Roll up in jellyroll fashion, starting with one of the short edges. Pinch the bottom seam to close to seal and tuck the ends under.

Place the dough in the loaf pans. Cover loosely with plastic wrap and let rise for 15 minutes, or until almost double in bulk.

Place the oven rack at the lower third position and pre-heat the oven to 190 degrees Celsius (175 degrees Celsius if using glass), for about 20 minutes.

Brush the loaves with the egg glaze. Bake for 20-25 minutes, or until the loaves are brown and the bottoms sound hollow when tapped with your finger. Remove from the pans and transfer to a rack to cool completely.

Winter Herb Bread

To make two loaves, you require:
Bakeware: Two 9×5-inch loaf pans

The herbs in this generously flecked bread make a dramatic flavour statement. Here's the sandwich bread at its best.

Ingredients

- 1 recipe milk bread dough
- 3 tablespoons minced fresh parsley (Ajmoda)
- 1 tablespoon crumbled dried basil leaves
- 1½ teaspoons dried dill weed
- 1½ teaspoons crumbled dried savoury
- 1½ teaspoons crumbled dried oregano or marjoram
- 1 teaspoon crushed dried tarragon leaves
- ½ teaspoon dried crumbled thyme

Method

Add the herbs to the dough during the mixing. Proceed to rise, shape and glaze and bake as directed in the recipe.

Cornmeal Stuffed Bread

To make this bread, you require:
Bakeware: 12×14-inch baking tray

Ingredients

- 1½ cups cornmeal flour
- ½ cup all-purpose flour
- 50 gm melted butter
- 1½ cups well blended sour curd
- 2 eggs

- 1 teaspoon sugar
- ½ teaspoon active dry yeast
- 1 teaspoon salt
- 1/8 cup warm water

Method

Assemble the ingredients and equipment around your work surface. Sprinkle the yeast and the sugar over the warm water in a small bowl. Stir to dissolve and let stand until foamy, for about 10 minutes.

You can make batter by hand and also by mixer.

To make by hand

Take the eggs in a bowl and beat the eggs well. Add the curd and butter to the eggs and beat the mixture well, taking care to avoid formation of lumps. Add the yeast mixture, cornmeal flour, sugar, salt, and all-purpose flour to the mixture slowly and beat this mixture for another 5 minutes to form a thick, consistent, homogeneous mixture.

To make by mixer

If using a heavy-duty electric mixer, fitted with the wire whip, combine all-purpose flour, cornmeal flour, sugar and salt in the work bowl. Add the yeast mixture, curd and butter to the dry mixture. Beat until smooth on medium low speed for 2-3 minutes.

Line a baking tray with oil and pour this mixture in the tray and let rise for about 3 minutes.

Pre-heat the oven at 12 degrees Celsius for about 2 minutes. Place the baking tray in the centre rack of the oven, and bake for about 15-20 minutes, or until golden brown in color.

> Cornmeal stuffed bread tastes delicious when served along with coriander chutney and tomato sauce.

Place the loaf on a cooling rack to cool. While the loaf is still warm, take a sharp knife and slice the loaf horizontally at the centre, with one end remaining still joined. Slowly, raise the upper half and spread butter, mustard or tomato sauce on the lower half. Then spread a thick layer of your favourite cooked vegetables. Seal the open three sides with cornflour paste. Envelope these loaves with aluminium foil and bake it in a pre-heated oven at 120 degrees Celsius for about 20 minutes.

Cool the stuffed bread on a cooling rack. Take a sharp knife, cut the loaf into pieces. The stuffed bread tastes delicious when served along with coriander chutney and tomato sauce.

wholewheat bread

Wholewheat bread is a baker's favourite! Many bakers feel that bread made with wheat flour is best from the point of view of taste and nutrition. The basic recipes call for a small proportion of wholewheat flour with a large amount of all-purpose flour for the proper gluten support. This bread differs significantly from all-white flour (Maida) in that the dough is denser and stickier and tends to rise slower.

Wheat flour is the major ingredient in yeast breads. In addition to being high in carbohydrates, it is cholesterol free and low in fat, depending on the added ingredients. Many types of wholewheat flour are now available for bread makers, including spelt and kamut, each with its own flavour, and various grinds of wholewheat from fine to coarse, which bake up into a wide spectrum of familiar and unique tastes and textures, ranging from nutty, bold, crunchy and fluffy to bland, woodsy, earthy and hearty. Never sift wholewheat flour. The coarse bits are an important part of the flour.

Wholegrain doughs tend to turn out much stiffer than doughs made with all-purpose flour. Hence, it requires a strong arm and good amount of kneading to thoroughly blend the ingredients and activate gluten properly. Hold back a full cup of flour, when you mix to adjust for the different water absorbing capacities of the flour. Add the reserved flour slowly to achieve the desired dough consistency. If the dough is too dry, add a bit more of water; if it is moist, add a little bit of the flour. Do resist adding too much extra flour during the kneading, as it will result in heavy and compact dough that will not bake properly in the centre. The dough should be very soft, almost sticky and a consistent one.

Rising Time must be strictly observed. If the dough over-rises the strands of the gluten, which are already limited, it can break, causing a flat-baked loaf. The right temperature is also important for the wholewheat loaves. If the oven is too hot, the crust will bake faster than the insides; if it's too cool, the loaf will be dry and dense.

Since the dough is soft, it needs a loaf pan to hold its shape. Even, pan rolls can be made. The dough, being too soft to hold its shape properly, is inappropriate for breading, but when made into a simple domed loaf, the finished bread stays moist and rises nicely. Clay loaf pans are the first choice for baking plain wholewheat breads; these pans produce a nice dark crust. For a crunchy bottom crust, you can sprinkle the greased pan with wheat germ, bran, coarse cornmeal or semolina on the bottom and on the sides.

Honey-Wholewheat Bread

This loaf is technically a light wholewheat, perfect for your first foray into wholegrain baking. It is a beautiful dough to work on. Depending upon the different grinds of the wholewheat flour, ranging from fine to coarse, different textures in the finished loaf are obtained. Be sure to knead only till the dough is soft and sticky; it will absorb the extra moisture during rising. Take care to shape the loaf properly so that you have a perfect final loaf with a nice, light texture.

To make two loaves, you require:
Bakeware: Two 8½×4½-inch loaf pans

Ingredients

- 2 cups warm water (40-45 degrees Celsius)
- 1 tablespoon active dry yeast
- Pinch of sugar
- ½ cup honey
- ¼ cup vegetable or olive oil
- 1 large egg
- ½ cup non-fat dry milk powder
- ½ cup instant potato flakes (dried potato pieces)
- 1½ cups wholewheat flour, stone ground, if possible
- 2¾-3¼ cups bread flour
- Melted butter for brushing (optional)

Method

Follow the steps given below carefully.

Step 1 – Mixing the Dough

Assemble the ingredients and the equipment. Pour ½ cup warm water into small bowl. Sprinkle the yeast and sugar over the surface. Stir to dissolve and let it stand at room temperature, for about 10 minutes, until foamy. Within a few minutes, the yeast will begin to bubble into thick foam and double or triple in volume. The batter can be made by hand and also my mixer.

To make by hand

Combine the remaining water, honey, oil, salt, egg, dry milk, potato flakes, and wholewheat flour in a large bowl. Using a balloon or a dough whisk beat vigorously for about 1 minute. Add the yeast mixture and ½ cup of all-purpose flour. Beat vigorously for about 1 minute more, until the dough is smooth. Switch over to using a wooden spoon, when the dough starts sticking to the whisk. Then add the remaining flour, little amount at a time, until soft, shaggy dough, that just clears the sides of the bowl, is formed.

To make by a mixer

If using a heavy-duty electric mixer, fit the paddle attachment, combine the remaining water, honey, oil, salt, egg, dry milk, potato flakes and the wholewheat flour in the work bowl. On medium-low speed, beat until smooth, for about one minute. Add the yeast mixture and half cup of the all-purpose flour. Switch to medium speed and beat for about one minute more. Switch back to low speed and add the remaining flour, half cup at a time, until a soft, shaggy dough, that just clears the sides of the bowl is formed.

Use a flour guard or a tea towel over the top to keep the flour from jumping out of the bowl. Switch to the dough hook when the dough thickens, about two-thirds through adding the flour, and knead for about 4 minutes on medium speed until the dough works its way up the hook. The dough will make a soft, slightly sticky ball and pull away from the sides of the bowl.

Step 2 – Kneading

Using a plastic dough card, turn the dough out onto a lightly floured work surface. Knead until firm yet still springy, less than one minute for a machine mixed dough (6-10 kneads to smooth it out) and 3-4 minutes for a hand-mixed dough, dusting with flour only one tablespoon at a time, just enough to prevent the dough from sticking to your hands and the work surface. This dough will be very smooth, yet retain a definite soft, slightly sticky quality, and never stiff.

Step 3 – Rising

Place the bowl in a greased deep container, grease the top and cover loosely with plastic wrap. If using the mixer, you can let the dough rise in the bowl and cover it with a plastic wrap. Mark the container to indicate how high the dough will be when it has risen. The dough should rise to double in volume, at room temperature in 1½-2 hours. The dough should not rise any higher than double in bulk.

Step 4 – Shaping the dough and the final rise

Lightly grease the bottom and the sides of the loaf pan. Turn the dough out onto a clean work surface; it will naturally deflate. Use little extra flour during shaping, otherwise the dough will dry out. Divide the dough into 2 equal portions with a metal scraper or knife. Pat each portion into a rectangle 8 inches long and 6 inches wide. Fold the short ends in one inch towards the middle to neaten. Beginning with the long end facing you, roll up the dough jellyroll fashion into a tight cylinder about the same length as your pan. Pinch the long seam to seal close. Place in the pan. The dough should be of even thickness and fill the pan and about two-thirds full. Cover loosely with plastic wrap. Repeat with the second portion. Let rise again at room temperature until the dough is fully double in bulk and about one inch over the rim of the pan in about 45 minutes-1 hour.

Pre-heat the oven to 175 degrees Celsius (160 degrees Celsius if using a glass pan) for about 20 minutes. Adjust the lower rack to the lower third position.

Gently brush the tops with melted butter, if desired. Place both the pans in the centre of the rack with plenty of space around each of them to allow proper heat circulation. It is during the first 15 minutes of baking when the dough reaches its maximum height and the wholewheat structure sets.

Bake for 30-35 minutes, or until the loaves are deep brown in colour, the sides have slightly shrunk away from the pan, and the bread sounds hollow when tapped on top with your finger. To be sure, you can insert a bamboo skewer into the centre of the loaf. If it comes out clean, it implies that the baking is complete. If the loaves are browning too fast, loosely tent (cover like a tent) with aluminium foil to enable the insides of the loaf to bake five to seven minutes longer.

Remove the loaf from the pan and peek underneath to check for even browning on the bottom. If it is too pale, remove the loaf from the pan and place it directly on the oven rack to bake for few more minutes. After taking the loaf from the pan, cool them on a rack.

Honey wholewheat bread stays moist for about 2 days. You can also store the unsliced bread wrapped in plastic food storage bag in the freezer for upto 2 months.

Rising Time must be strictly observed. If the dough over-rises the strands of the gluten, which are already limited, it can break, causing a flat-baked loaf.

Molasses Gram Bread

Substitute 1½ cups gram flour for 1½ cups of wheat flour. Substitute ½ cup light molasses for the honey. The preparation method remains the same like Honey wholewheat bread.

Masala Bread

Add chopped onions, fresh coriander, green chopped chillies, chopped ginger, fresh chopped mint, to the Honey whole-wheat bread dough, proof and then bake.

Garlic Bread

Add some garlic powder and some pieces of fresh, chopped garlic to the Honey wholewheat bread dough and proceed to bake.

Honey Wholewheat Pan Rolls

Honey wholewheat bread dough bakes up into a nice variety of dinner-rolls. The shaping is easy and fun-giving, and the piping hot rolls are as moist as if they were made with all white flour. The dough should be kept as soft as possible. Serve the rolls hot so that the butter melts immediately into them.

To make 32 rolls, you require:
Bakeware: Two 9-inch round cake pans, oven-proof glass or disposable aluminium foil pans

Ingredients

- One recipe Honey wholewheat bread dough
- 8 tablespoons butter, melted

Method

Prepare the dough through the end of step 3 (Given in the page 88). Grease the bottom and side of the two round pans.

To shape the rolls, turn the dough out onto a work surface and divide it in half. Divide each portion into 16 pieces roll each into 2 to 2½-inch balls. Dip each one into the melted butter and place in the pans, 16 in each pan, letting the balls just touch one another. Cover loosely with plastic wrap and let rise at room temperature until double in bulk, for about 40 minutes. Place the oven rack in the middle position and pre-heat the oven to 190 degrees Celsius (175 degrees Celsius, if using glass pans).

Brush the tops with melted butter, so that they will be soft. Bake for about 25 minutes or until golden brown and the surface is dry to touch. Slide the pan rolls out of the pan onto a wire rack, to cool. The rolls taste best when served hot.

Honey Wholewheat Bread with Rice

To make two loaves, your require:
Bakeware: Two 8½ x4½-inch loaf pans

Ingredients

- ½ cup brown or white rice
- 1 cup water
- 1 recipe honey wholewheat bread dough

Method

Place the rice in the deep bowl and add cold water to cover. Swirl with your finger, drain in a fine-mesh sieve, and rinse under cold running water. Repeat a few times until foam no longer rises to the surface during the rinsing.

In a saucepan over high heat, bring the water to a boil. Add the rice, reduce the heat as slow as possible and cover. Cool until all the water is absorbed and the rice is tender, about 20 minutes. Let stand, uncovered until it comes down at room temperature. The rice will be around 1 cup in volume.

Add the rice to the dough with water after adding the potato flakes. Proceed to mix, knead, rise, shape and bake as directed in the recipe.

Honey Wholewheat Seed Bread

To make two loaves, your require:
Bakeware: Two 8½×4 ½-inch loaf pans.

Ingredients

- 1 recipe Honey-wholewheat bread dough
- ¾ cup sunflower seeds
- 1/3 cup whole millet
- 3 tablespoons poppy seeds
- 3 tablespoons flax seeds

Add the seeds with whole-wheat flour. Proceed to mix, rise, and shape; rise again, and bake as directed in the recipe.

Cranberry and Cinnamon Wholewheat Bread

Dried cranberries (*Karanda*, in reality it is a 'Natal Plum')
are a very good alternative to raisins, and are easily available.

To make two loaves, you require:
Bakeware: Two 8½×4½ -inch loaf pans.

Ingredients

- 1 tablespoon ground cinnamon
- 1 recipe Honey-Wholewheat Bread dough
- 1½ cups dried cranberries

Lightly grease the bottom and the sides of the two loaf pans and
set aside. Add one-tablespoon ground cinnamon with the wholewheat flour. Mix, knead and rise the dough through step 3
(Given in the page 88).

To shape the dough divide it in half and pat each portion into
an 8×6-inch rectangle and sprinkle each with half of the dried
cranberries. Press them into the dough and roll up jelly-roll
fashion from the long edge. Pinch the seams to seal and place,
seam side down, in the loaf pans. Proceed to rise and bake
as directed in the recipe.

holiday sweet bread

...Holiday sweet breads are meant to be a treat to both taste and looks. These fragmented tasty creations never go out of style.

Holidays are a time when the most timid and lazy bakers fire up their ovens. They are an opportunity to highlight and display those coveted family recipes or ones taken from friends and neighbours for their favourite homemade loaves. Eating beautifully-shaped holiday bread is an integral part of western holiday tradition. These breads give great pleasure, not only to the baker, but to the person eating it as well.

While daily breads are low in fat and sugar, holiday baking is the time to pull out all the stops; holiday sweet breads are meant to be luxurious in both taste and texture. These fragrant, yeasty creations never go out of style. They can be served at breakfast with tea and fresh fruit, with coffee or desserts, or for a special celebration with a dessert wine. While those breads are mostly associated with holidays, there is no such hard and fast rule. They can be made as when one desires.

Once you make a basic sweet holiday yeast dough, you can make anything from the Italian dove-shaped Easter cake called La Colomba di Pasqua, to the Russian pretzel-shaped loaf called Krendl, to the domed Italian Panettone, to a round Norwegian Julekage, all with relative ease. Don't feel awesome by the foreign names – the breads have been named after some story incorporating religion, history, artistry and even fantasy, from their respective countries.

All the sweet doughs are minor variations of the same basic proportions, though the fillings and shapes create distinctively different breads. They have fruit, nuts, spices, cheese fillings and flavourings; are sometimes splashed with intensely flavoured liquors; and reveal beautiful patterns when cut. Do keep a variety of dried fruits, poppy seeds, dried powdered lemon peel, nut flours and whole nuts in the freezer. You can make glazed dried fruit to use in place of less flavoured commercial candied fruit. A good quality vanilla, the Queen of Spices, is essential. It is a primary ingredient in sweet breads, because it blends so well with other spices when combined with sugar, it gives a boost to the dough's flavour on the whole. Keep pure vanilla, almond, hazel nut, and other extracts, as well as lemon and orange oils, refrigerated.

This master recipe takes the same amount of time to prepare as a regular loaf of bread:

- You just need to leave the dough softer.
- Always use a light hand and handle this dough as little as possible when shaping.
- Gently rework the dough, if you are not satisfied with the shape you have framed.
- Simply allow the dough to rest on the work surface, covered with plastic wrap for about 10 minutes, then reform.

This short rest gives the gluten proteins in the dough a chance to relax. Since the dough will rise almost double during the last rise and then, with help from the eggs, will double again in the oven, detailed and intricate shapes and decorations do not hold their form when baked. Consequently, experiment a little bit, until you get the shape you want.

You can shape the dough in as many ways you like. You can fashion it into one large bread, and glaze it with a vanilla-powdered sugar glaze. You can also give shapes from dome rounded wreaths, to heart-shaped small mounds that reflect centuries of bread-making tradition. Use of decorative moulds to vary the shapes can also be done.

The final decorative touches include glazing, frosting and garnishing. Glazing is an important finishing touch on sweet breads; brushing on milk mixed with sugar, egg yolks mixed with some milk, or egg whites with cold water, gives a glossy visual appeal and glues on the coarse sugar crystals. A simple frosting, based on powdered sugar mixed with milk until pourable or spreadable gives a lively topping of concentrated sweetness and a very pretty, delectable finish.

You can garnish the sweet breads with drizzled icing and decorations. You can top them with sugar-coated rose petals, silver-coated almonds, nuts, candied fruit, maple sugar, and candy shaped into maple loaves, coarse shredded coconut, cherry halves, chocolate-dipped dried fruit, while the glaze is still wet. They will adhere to as it dries. You can even use those teeth-shattering tiny silver balls called dragees, dotting the top. Large crystal decorating sugar, which comes in fetching pastel colours, can also be used. Coarse and sprinkling sugars need to be sprinkled before baking to make a crunchy, sweet crust.

Components for Holiday Sweet Breads

Here are some basic ingredients called for in the recipes to add to your holiday sweet breads.

Honey-glazed dried fruit

To make about 8 ounces (1 ounce = 28 gms), you require:

Ingredients

- 1¼ cups granulated sugar
- 1¼ cup honey
- 2 tablespoons light corn syrup
- 1/3 cup water
- 8 ounces dry fruits such as dry apricots, pineapple, figs or pear halves

In a deep heavy saucepan, make syrup by combining sugar, honey, corn syrup, and water. Heat over low heat, stirring constantly with a wooden spoon, until the sugar dissolves, about three minutes. Using metal tongs, place the fruit in the syrup, taking care not to splash. Bring the mixture to a low boil without stirring. Immediately reduce the heat and simmer. Cook the fruit slowly for 15 minutes exactly, stirring gently to avoid burning of the syrup. The fruit will plump up.

Remove the pan from the heat and place it immediately in a pan full of tap water to cool the syrup slightly. Carefully remove the individual pieces of fruit with the tongs, letting the extra syrup drip back into the pan. Place them on a layer of parchment paper set on a wire rack to cool completely at room temperature, at least 8 hours.

Store in an airtight plastic container with the glazed fruit in layers separated by clean layers of parchment paper that has been slightly sprayed with a thin film of vegetable cooking oil. Some of the fruits can be rolled in sifted powdered sugar for a pretty presentation. You can store them upto 3 weeks in the refrigerator.

Vanilla-powdered sugar glaze

About 1 cup, enough for 1 over-sized bread,
2 large loaves, 2 coffee cakes,
or 1 dozen cinnamon rolls.

This is the basic sweet glaze used for topping cinnamon buns and dripping loaves. Glazing is done, usually when the baked loaf is slightly warm. If a loaf is to be frozen, always glaze after defrosting.

- 1 cup sifted, fine-powdered sugar
- 1 tablespoon melted, unsalted butter
- 2-3 tablespoons hot milk
- 1 teaspoon pure vanilla extract

Combine the ingredients in a small bowl and whisk until smooth. Adjust the consistency of the glaze by adding more milk, few drops at a time. Place the loaf on a wire rack with the sheet of parchment paper or a plate underneath for easy clean-up. Using a large spoon, drizzle with a back and forth motion over the top of the loaf. Arrange any nuts or fruits on top. As the glaze cools, it will set up.

Almond: Substitute 1 teaspoon pure almond extract for the vanilla.

Hazelnut: Substitute 1 teaspoon pure hazelnut extract for the vanilla.

Lemon: Substitute fresh lemon juice for the milk and omit the vanilla.

Orange: Substitute fresh orange juice for the milk.

Sweet Spice: Add ½ teaspoon ground cinnamon, cardamom, or nutmeg.

Home-made almond paste

Make about two cups.

Almond paste is a good staple to have on hand for topping or filling breads and pastries. It can be made at home very quickly.

To make about 2 cups, you require:
- 2 cups sliver blanched almonds
- 2 cups powdered sugar
- ¼th cup water
- 2 tablespoons light corn syrup
- 1½ teaspoons almond extract

In a work bowl of the food processor, fitted with a metal blade, process the almonds with ½ cup of the powdered sugar until finely ground and process briefly. Combine the water, corn syrup and almond extract in a measuring cup and add through the feed tube while the machine is running. Process until smooth and the mixture forms a ball. You can use immediately or refrigerate up to two weeks or put it in the freezer for a longer period of time.

You can also take hazel nut instead of the almonds to make hazel nut paste.

Here is egg rich sweet bread dough that serves as the master recipe for a variety of sweet breads, each one unique in itself. It is quick to make and very easy to handle. It is shaped simply into pan loaves, a shape you will be comfortable with by now. You can serve with coffee and fresh fruit, or simply alone by itself.

To make two loaves, you require:
Bakeware: Two 9×5-inch loaf pans

Ingredients

- ½ cup milk
- 8 tablespoons unsalted butter
- 1 tablespoon active dry yeast
- Pinch of sugar
- ¾ cup warm water (40-45 degrees Celsius)
- 5 to 5½ cups all-purpose flour
- 1/3 cup sugar
- Grated zest of 2 lemons
- 1½ teaspoons salt
- 3 large eggs
- 2 teaspoons pure vanilla extract

For Fruit Mix

- 1 cup chopped mixed candied fruit or honey-glazed dry fruit
- ½ cup silvered almonds
- Vanilla or almond powdered sugar glaze

Method

Follow the steps given below carefully.

Step 1 – Mixing the Dough

Assemble the ingredients and equipment around your work surface. Combine the milk and butter in a small saucepan and heat until the butter is melted. Let it cool for about 20 minutes. Sprinkle the yeast and pinch of sugar over the warm water in a small bowl. Stir to dissolve and let it stand until foamy for about 10 minutes. You can make batter by hand and also by mixer.

To make by hand

Combine 1½ cups of the flour, sugar, lemon zest and salt in a large bowl. Add the yeast and milk mixtures, eggs and vanilla.

First stage of mixing dough by hand

Using a balloon or dough whisk beat until creamy for about 2 minutes, scraping the bowl occasionally. Add ½ cup of the flour and beat vigorously for 2 minutes. Switch to a wooden spoon when the dough clogs the whisk. Add the remaining flour, ½ cup at a time; beating for 2 minutes more to make the soft dough that just clears the sides of the bowl.

To make by mixer

If using heavy-duty electric mixer fitted with the paddle attachment, combine 1½ cups of the flour, sugar, lemon zest and salt in the work bowl. Add the yeast and milk mixtures, egg and vanilla. Beat until smooth on medium-low speed, about 2 minutes. Add 1 cup flour and beat 1 minute more. Switch to low speed and add the remaining flour, ½ cup at a time, until soft dough that clears the side of the bowl is formed.

Use the flour guard or drape a tea towel over the top to keep the flour from jumping out of the bowl. Switch to the dough hook when dough thickens, when about two-thirds of the flour has been added, and knead for 2 minutes on medium speed, or until the dough works its way up the hook. The dough will make a soft ball, pull away from the sides of the bowl and roll around.

Step 2 – Kneading

Using a plastic dough card, turn the dough out onto a lightly-floured work surface. Knead until firm yet smooth and satiny, under 1 minute for a machine-mixed dough (6-10 kneads to smooth it out) and 3-4 minutes for a hand-mixed dough, dusting with flour, only 1 tablespoon at a time, as needed to prevent the dough from sticking to your hands and work surface.

Step 3 – Rising

Place the dough ball in a greased, deep container, turn over once to grease the top, and cover with plastic wrap. If using the mixer, you can put on the cover to let the dough rise in the bowl itself. Mark the container to indicate how high the dough will be when it has risen to double in volume. Let rise at room temperature, until double in bulk, about 2 hours. Do not rush this dough, the full rising time is important to develop the optimum flavour and texture.

Step 4 – Adding the fruit mix, shaping the dough and the final rise

Turn the dough out onto a clean surface; it will naturally deflate. Pat the dough out to shape into a large rectangle. Sprinkle the dough evenly with the fruits and nuts. Fold the dough over to enclose the ingredients and knead lightly to distribute evenly.

Lightly grease the bottom and sides of two 9×5-inch loaf pans. Use a metal bench scraper or a knife to divide the dough into 2 equal portions. Peel each portion into a pan loaf by shaping the dough into 8×6-inch rectangles. Fold the 2 opposite short ends 1 inch into the middle to neaten.

Beginning with the long edge facing, you roll up the dough in jellyroll fashion into a tight cylinder about the same length as your pan. Pinch the long seam to seal close. Place the loaf in the pan. The log should be of an even thickness and fill the pan about two-thirds full. Cover loosely with a plastic wrap

Repeat the same process with the second portion. Let rise at room temperature, until the dough is fully double in bulk and about 1 inch over the rims of the pans, about 45 minutes.

Step 5 – Baking, glazing, cooling and storage

Twenty minutes before baking place the oven rack in the middle of the oven and preheat the oven to 175 degrees Celsius (160 degrees Celsius if using glass).

Bake for about 45-50 minutes or until the loaves are deep golden brown, the sides have slightly shrunk away from the pan, and the bread sounds hollow when tapped on the top or bottom with your fingers. An instant read thermometer would read 90-95 degree Celsius, when inserted in the loaf. Also check for an even browning on the bottom. If it is too pale, remove the loaf from the pan and place it directly on the oven rack for a few minutes more or bake in the pan longer in the lowest position in the oven.

When the baking is completed, remove the loaves from the pans and place them on a wire rack to cool. Meanwhile, prepare the glaze.

Place the rack with the warm bread on it over a large plate or sheet of parchment paper to catch the drips. Using a large spoon, drizzle the warm loaf with the glaze, letting it drip down the sides. Loaves are best served at room temperature.

Holiday sweet bread stays moist for about 2 days. Store the unsliced bread wrapped in a plastic storage bag at room temperature. It can stay fresh in the freezer unglazed for upto 2 months. Defrost on the day needed, still wrapped, adding the final glazing, decorative touches or a dusting of powdered sugar at that time. The loaf will taste and slice as perfectly as was on the day it was baked.

Holiday sweet bread stays moist for about 2 days. Store the unsliced bread wrapped in a plastic storage bag at room temperature.

Pannetone with an almond crust

The *Italian pannetone* is probably the most famous holiday bread. Pannetone is baked in a round mould (free-form rounds work just as well, though they don't end up as tall). You can use a charlotte pan, paper moulds, or a tall smooth tube pannetone. In the Italian tradition, this bread is served with chilled Asti Spunmante, an Italian sparkling wine.

To make 1 large or 2 small round loaves, you require:
Bakeware: One 7½-inch diameter round mould. Two 5½-inch pannetone moulds or one 11×17-inch baking sheet

Ingredients

- 1 recipe Holiday Sweet Bread dough
- ½ cup minced dried apricots
- 1/3 cup dried cherries
- 1/3 cup golden raisins
- 3 tablespoons slivered almonds
- 3 tablespoons pine nuts
- 1½ teaspoons crushed aniseed
- 1½ tablespoons all-purpose flour

For Almond paste topping

- ½ cup almond paste
- 1 large egg white, beaten
- 2 tablespoons sugar

Method

Grease a 7½-inch round mould, or line an 11×17-inch baking sheet with parchment pepper. The paper pannetone needs no greasing; place both on a baking sheet. Prepare the dough through the end of step 3 (Given in the page 102).

To shape the dough, turn it out onto the work surface and pat it out into a flat shape. Dust the fruits, nuts, and aniseed with the flour, and sprinkle over the surface of the dough. Fold the dough over, press it gently, and knead to distribute evenly. Form into 1 or 2 round loaves by first pressing the dough into a thick round. Then tuck the edges into the centre, until a firm, round shape is formed. The round should be perfectly even and have no tears or breaks in the surface. If making 1 loaf, place in the round mould. If making 2 loaves, place in the paper moulds and set on the baking sheet. If making two free-form loaves, place them on the baking sheet, at least 4 inches apart. Loosely cover with plastic wrap and let rise at room temperature, until almost double in bulk, 45 to 60 minutes.

Using a hand-held electric mixer, beat together the almond paste, egg white, and sugar until smooth and fluffy. Pre-heat the oven at 175 degrees Celsius for about 20 minutes.

Spread the top of the pannetone with a coating of the almond paste topping. There is no need to worry, if it drips down a bit. With a small sharp knife, gently slash a deep 'X' into the top of the dough. Bake for 40 to 45 minutes (the smaller loaves will take 8 to 10 minutes less) at the lower third position of the oven, until golden brown and a cake tester comes out clean when inserted into the centre. Remove from the oven and transfer to a wire rack to cool completely before slicing.

Kulich

Kulich is a Russian yeast cake served at year-round celebrations and Orthodox Easter. It has a tall shape rather like a puffy mushroom, which is decorated with strips of dough on the top, forming the initial 'X', signifying that Christ is risen. As for an easier alternative, you can simply slash an 'X' on the top.

To make two 7-inch round loaves, you require:
Bakeware: Two 6½-inch diameter round moulds or two 500 ml coffee cans.

Ingredients

- 1 recipe homemade sweet bread dough
- ¼ cup golden raisins
- ¼ cups dried sweet cherries
- 3 tablespoons lemon-flavoured vodka or dry white wine.
- ¼ cup finely chopped candid lemon peel
- 1/3 cup chopped pistachios
- ¼ cup crystallised ginger, finely chopped
- 1 tablespoon melted unsalted butter for brushing
- 2 tablespoons powdered sugar for dusting

Method

In a small bowl, combine the raisins, cherries and vodka. Let it stand at room temperature for 30 minutes to grind and soften.

Prepare the dough through the end of step 3 (Given in the page 102). Grease well the two round moulds or two coffee cans. If using two round moulds, fasten a 4-inch high aluminium foil collar onto the top on the mould.

To shape the dough, turn it out onto a clean work surface, it will naturally deflate. Pat it out into a large rectangle, sprinkle evenly with the macerated fruit, the lemon peel, pistachios and chopped ginger. Fold the dough over and knead gently to distribute evenly. Divide the dough into 2 equal portions. Knead into a ball. Place each ball in the moulds, filling no more than two-thirds full. Cover loosely with buttered plastic wrap and let rise until even with the rim of the moulds for about 40 minutes.

Pre-heat the oven at 175 degrees Celsius for about 20 minutes. Bake the moulds in the lower third position for about 35 to 40 minutes or until golden brown. You can also insert a cake tester or skewer into the centre to check, whether the bread has been baked or not.

If the top browns too quickly, you can tent the tops loosely with a piece of aluminium foil. As soon as the baking is completed, slide the baked loaves out of their moulds onto a wire rack to cool.

Kulich has a tall shape rather like a puffy mushroom, which is decorated with strips of dough on the top.

Brush the warm tops with melted butter and dust with powdered sugar sprinkled from a mesh sieve. Cool completely and serve at room temperature.

To serve, cut off the top puff horizontally and place it on a serving plate. Then slice horizontally down from top into ½-inch thick slices, so that the kulich gradually diminishes in height. Arrange the top half at the centre of the plate, and the other halves around it.

Scandinavian Holiday Sweet Bread

Perfumed with cardamom, this holiday bread shows up in some form or another in every Scandinavian country.

You can add a bit of rye flour to give a slightly different taste and texture.

In Norway, this fancy Christmas sweet bread is known as *Julekage* and is always made in round loaves. It has two finishing glazes; one brushed on before baking and one after. Hazelnut extract can be substituted for the vanilla extract in the dough if you are making the hazelnut glaze.

To make two round loaves, you require:
Bakeware: One 11×17×1-inch baking sheet or two 9-inch pans.

Ingredients

1 recipe holiday sweet bread with 1 cup rye flour substituted for 1 cup of all purpose flour and 1½ teaspoons grounded cardamom substituted for the lemon zest.

- 1 cup coarsely chopped mixed candied fruit or honey-glazed dry fruit
- 1 cup dried currants or dried cranberries
- 2 tablespoons all-purpose flour
- 1 egg beaten with 1 tablespoon milk for glaze
- 2 tablespoons coarse sugar or decorating sugar
- Hazelnut or cardamom powdered sugar glaze.

Method

Line a baking sheet with parchment paper or grease two 9-inch cake pans. Prepare the dough through the end step 3 (Given in the page 102).

To shape the dough, turn it out onto the work-station and pat into a flat shape. Dust the fruit and currants with the flour and sprinkle over the surface of the dough. Fold the dough over, press in gently and knead to distribute evenly.

Cover the dough ball with the plastic wrap on the work surface and let rest for 10 minutes to relax the dough.

Divide the dough into 2 even portions. Form into round loaves by pressing the dough into a thick round. Then knead the edges into the centre, pulling from the underside to create a thick round. Then knead the edges into the centre, pulling from the underside to create surface tension as you press into the centre. Turn; folding into the centre, until a taut, firm round, with its smooth side on the work surface is formed.

The rounds should be perfectly even with no tears or breaks in the surface. Place on the baking sheet, at least 4 inches apart, or in the cake pans. Loosely cover with a plastic wrap and let rise at room temperature until double in bulk, 45 to 60 minutes. Brush the dough with the egg glaze and sprinkle with sugar.

Pre-heat the oven at 175 degrees Celsius for about 20 minutes. Place the baking sheet at the lower third of the oven and bake for about 40-45 minutes, until golden brown and a cake tester comes out clean when inserted into the centre of the loaf. Remove from the oven and transfer to a wire rack.

Place the rack over a sheet of parchment paper or a large plate to catch the drips. Prepare the glaze and drizzle the warm loaf, in a back and forth motion with cardamom sugar glaze.

Let it cool completely to set the glaze before slicing.

Three King's Bread

In Mexico, Christmas is celebrated two times a year, once with the traditional birth of Jesus, and the other with the arrival of the Three Wise Men with gifts for the baby.

Today, the loving parents leave the toys and gifts for their children, carrying on the tradition. The special food for this occasion is the Rosca de Reyes, the King's bread ring. If you find the whole almond in the bread, you will be crowned king of the festivities. The bread can also be decorated by setting a small crown cut out of gold foil in the centre of the bread baked wreath and serve with Mexican hot chocolate.

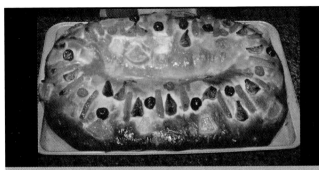

To make 1 loaf, you require:
Bakeware: One 11×17-inch baking sheet or 11-inch ceramic ring mould.

Ingredients

- 1 recipe holiday sweet bread with 1½ teaspoons grounded cinnamon added with sugar
- 2 cups coarsely chopped mixed candid fruit or honey-glazed dry fruit
- ½ cup chopped pitted dates
- 1 egg beaten with 1 tablespoon milk for glaze
- 1 whole almond, inserted for the prize
- 14 raw sugar cubes
- ½ teaspoon ground cinnamon

Method

Line a baking sheet with parchment paper to grease the ring mould. Prepare the dough through the end of step 3 (Given in the page 102).

To shape the dough, turn it out onto the work surface and pat into a large rectangle. Sprinkle with the fruit and dates. Press in gently, then knead to distribute evenly. Cover the dough ball with plastic wrap on the work surface and let rest for 10 minutes to relax the dough.

Divide the dough into 2 uneven portions. Roll the larger section into a fat rope about 16 inches long. Place on a baking sheet and bring the ends together to form a ring. Using the back of a knife, mark 8 indentations around the ring at even intervals. Brush the circle with egg glaze. Divide the remaining section of dough into 8 even pieces and form into balls. Press a whole almond into one dough ball from beneath. Use your fingers to pry open each indentations and set a ball of dough into each one. Press to adhere and brush again with egg glaze. The remaining egg glaze can be refrigerated if left

Pressing almond into centre of dough ball

Spreading open indentation so dough ball can be seated in opening

unused. Cover loosely with the plastic wrap and let rise at room temperature until puffy, for about 30 minutes. Pre-heat the oven at 175 degrees Celsius for about 20 minutes.

Crush sugar cubes and mix in a small bowl with cinnamon. Brush the dough with more egg glaze and sprinkle with the crushed sugar. Bake the dough in the lower third of the oven, for about 25 to 30 minutes, or until golden brown and firm to touch. Cool on the wire rack before serving at room temperature.

Russian Krendl

Russian Krendl is a wonderful fruit-filled, pretzel like bread, used not only just for Birthdays and Christening celebrations as the Russians, but also with afternoon tea instead of cake.

To make 1 loaf, you require:
Bakeware: One 11×17-inch baking sheet.

Ingredients

For Apple filling, you need

- 1 recipe Holiday sweet bread dough
- 2 tablespoons unsalted butter
- 4 medium golden delicious apples, peeled, cored and chopped
- 2 tablespoons sugar
- 1 teaspoon ground cinnamon
- ¾ cup chopped pitted prunes (can also use plums)
- ¾ cup dried apricots
- Lemon-powdered sugar glaze
- 3 tablespoons sliced almonds

Preparation of filing

Melt the butter in a heavy-base pan and add the apples. Cook over medium-high heat for 1 minute. Sprinkle with sugar and cinnamon and continue to cook until tender, a few minutes more. Remove from the heat. Add the prunes and apricots. Cool, till the filling is warm to touch.

Method

Line a baking sheet with parchment paper. Prepare the dough through the end of step 3 (Given in the page 102).

To shape the dough, turn it out into a lightly floured work surface and, with a rolling-pin; roll out into a rectangle 10 inches wide and 30 inches long. With a rubber spatula, spread the filling over the dough, leaving a 2-inch border all the way around. Starting from the long edge, roll up the dough into a jellyroll fashion. Pinch the bottom seam to seal. Carefully lay across the baking sheet. Holding one end in each hand, cross the dough, once or twice, at the ends, creating one large loop of dough with the ends twisted together. Pull the twisted end up and over the loop of dough, placing the twisted end in the centre of the circle on the bottom. You will have a pretzel shape. Place it on the baking sheet. Cover loosely with plastic wrap and let rise at room temperature until puffy, for about 30 minutes.

Pre-heat the oven to 175 degrees Celsius for about 20 minutes. Place the baking sheet in the middle of the oven. Bake for about 45 to 55 minutes, or until brown and firm to touch.

Remove from the oven and slide with the parchment paper onto a wire rack. Prepare the glaze and drizzle the warm loaf with the entire glaze, letting it drip down the sides. Immediately sprinkle with sliced almonds while the glaze is still wet. Let the loaf cool completely to set the glaze before slicing.

Italian Bread Carp and Doves

The whimsical shapes of a carp (fresh-water fish) with almond scales and a dove are found throughout the European continent to celebrate the baker's art and skill. The fat dove, known as a Colomba in Italian, is the bird of peace. The fish is an early symbol of fertility and Christianity.

To make 1 large carp & 2 medium doves, you require:
Bakeware: Two 11x17-inch baking sheets.

Ingredients

- 1 recipe Holiday sweet bread dough
- 1 egg beaten with 1-teaspoon water for glaze
- 1 cup whole blanched almonds split in half
- 4 large dried currants or dried cranberries

Method

Line 2 baking sheets with parchment paper. Prepare the dough though the end of step 3 (page 102).

To shape the dough, turn it out onto a lightly-floured work surface and divide into 2 equal portions.

Shaping the carp

To form the carp, roll out one portion into a ¾-inch thick rectangle. Using a pastry wheel cut out a large oval, using the entire rectangle. Combine and re-roll the scrapes; cut out a small fin and a triangular tailpiece. Using the back of a knife make parallel lines across the fins ad the tail. Coil a small scrap to make an eye and form another into small crescen for the mouth. Brush the entire surface of the oval with the egg glaze and then place the tail, fin, eye and mouth on the body. Brush the entire carp with another layer of egg glaze Using kitchen shears, make 'V' shape marks at 1-2-inch intervals on two-thirds of the fish's back to make scales. The cuts made by the scissors should not be so deep, which touch the bottom of the dough.

Press a split almond half into each scale, cured side up, so that it lies flat on the body with most of the almond showing .Carefully transfer the carp to the baking sheet. Cover loosely with plastic wrap and let rise at room temperature until double, in about 45 minutes.

Shaping the doves

To form the doves, lightly re-dust the work surface with the flour. Roll out the second portion of the dough into a ¾-inch thick rectangle. Using a pastry wheel cut off 2 strips of dough 1½ to 2 inches wide from one of the long sides. Using you palms, roll each strip into a log about 12 inches long. Tie each log into such a way that the one end becomes the tail and the other end becomes the beak of the dove. The tailpiece is the larger end, extending about 2 inches. (As shown in the picture). Shape the beak into a pointed one.

Cut several gashes into the tailpiece with shears to form a farmed-out section to represent feathers. With the help of the back of the knife, make parallel lines on these feathers. Brush the dove gently with the egg glaze and place a currant or a dried cranberry on each side of the head for the eyes. In the same way, make another dove. Place the doves on the second baking sheet. Cover loosely with a plastic wrap and let rise at room temperature until double, in about 45 minutes.

Preheat the oven to 175 degrees Celsius for about 20 minutes.

Brush the carp with another coat of egg glaze and place the baking sheet at the middle side of the oven. Bake for about 25 to 30 minutes.

Snipping "scales" into fish

Place the carp onto a cooling rack. Place the doves in the centre rack of the oven and bake to about 175 degrees Celsius. After 15 minutes, i.e., halfway through baking, cover the heads and tailpieces with foil, shiny side up, to keep them from excessive browning, while the body completes baking. Bake again for about 15 minutes, or until golden brown. Transfer the doves onto a wire rack to cool.

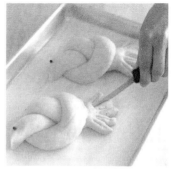

Using back of knife to press lines into dove tails

a flat bread

Flatbreads are one of the first breads ever made at home as well as one of the easiest to make. Coming from the Latin word *focus*, or hearth, focaccia, Italian flat bread was considered a daily bread in the ancient world before the invention of the closed oven.

Flatbreads are known by various names in different countries. In Umbria and *Tuscany*, focaccia is called *Schiacciata*, in Emilia, it is called *Piadina*, in Sicily, and it is called *Sfincione*. In France, it is known as *Fougasse*.

Focaccia is identical and proportional to pizza dough – just flour, salt, yeast and liquid and olive oil for flavour. The difference between focaccia and pizza dough lies in the thickness and simplicity of the toppings. Instead of being baked immediately after shaping to form a thin crisp, focaccia dough is left to rise a second time.

Focaccia is favourite summer bread, and the bread for you to use your imagination. A pan of risen focaccia dotted with olive oil, is one of the prettiest sights in the bread world. You can simply do it with dried or fresh herbs marinated in good olive oil, add nuts to the dough or use as a topping, make different shapes, or even add sugar and top with sliced fruit for a sweet breakfast version.

Focaccia is often topped with only olive oil and salt. Toppings like mushroom, cheese and onions are meant to be scattered lightly as flavour enhancers and not as generously like pizza toppings. Flat breads can also be enhanced with sugar, honey, spices, dried and fresh fruit. In Italy, during the grape harvest season, fresh grapes are pressed into the dough.

Focaccia makes a simple yet satisfying appetiser or sandwich bread when cut horizontally, or it can be cut into chunks to be served along with roasted meats and salads. It is best eaten the same day it is baked, preferably right out of the oven.

Olive oil is an important ingredient in flat breads. It brings out the other flavours, while still giving the bread a rich buttery texture.

The general rule is to use a good quality pure or virgin olive oil when needed for the ingredient list and extra virgin olive oil for dipping and pouring over bread, where the unique character flavour and aroma can be best appreciated.

Use a large baking sheet with a rim since the dough will rise to about 1½ inches high. You can even use a 14-inch deep dish pizza pan. If you use a smaller pan than what is called for, the focaccia will be thicker.

Focaccia with herbs and garlic

This is a firm focaccia dough, which is easier for the beginners to work with, than the standard dough, which is extremely soft. Use of fat free milk instead of water gives a better flavour to the focaccia. Avoid use of whole cream milk.

To make about 1 rectangular or round flat bread to serve about 10 people, you require:
Bakeware: One 11×17-inch rectangular baking sheet or a 14-inch deep dish pizza pan.

Ingredients

- 2 teaspoons active dry yeast
- Pinch of sugar
- 3-3½ cups all-purpose flour
- 1-1/3 cups warm fat-free milk (40-45 degrees Celcius)
- 1½ teaspoons salt
- 1/3 cup good quality olive oil.

For herb topping

- ¼ cup good quality olive oil
- 3 cloves garlic sliced very thin
- 1 tablespoon crushed dried sage leaves or 3 tablespoons finely chopped fresh sage leaves.
- 1 tablespoon crushed dried basil or 3 tablespoons finely chopped fresh basil leaves.
- Yellow corn meal flour for sprinkling in the pan.
- Salt for sprinkling over the focaccia.

Method

Follow the steps given below carefully.

Step 1 – Mixing the Dough

Assemble the ingredients and equipment around your work surface. In a work bowl, sprinkle the yeast, sugar and one tablespoon of the flour over the milk. Stir till dissolved, and let stand until foamy, about 15 minutes. The batter can be made by hand and also by mixer.

To make by hand

Combine one cup of the flour and the salt in a large bowl and make a well. Pour the yeast mixture and olive oil into the well and stir to combine. Using a balloon or dough whisk beat vigorously for 2 minutes, adding the remaining flour ½ cup at a time, until a sticky dough is formed, which pulls away from the sides of the bowl.

To make by mixer

If using a heavy-duty electric mixer fitted with paddle attachment, combine one cup of the flour and salt in the work bowl and make a well. Pour in the yeast mixture and olive oil and stir on low speed to combine. On low speed, beat for one minute. Add the remaining flour, ¼ cup at a time, until soft, smooth dough that just clears the sides of the bowl is formed. Add the flour slowly to keep it jumping out of the bowl. Switch to the dough hook when the dough thickens, about two-thirds through adding the flour, and knead for about 2 minutes on medium speed. The dough should be very soft.

Step 2 – Kneading

Using a plastic dough card, turn the dough out into a lightly work surface. Knead until the dough is smooth and is able to hold its own shape, dusting with flour only one tablespoon at a time, just enough to prevent the dough from sticking to your hands and the work surface. The dough should stay as soft as possible, smooth and very springy. Form it into a flattened ball.

Step 3 – Rising and making the topping

Place the dough ball in a greased, deep container and cover with a plastic wrap. If using the mixer, you can put on the cover to let the dough rise in the bowl itself. Let rise at room temperature until triple in bulk, about 1½ hours.

If you plan to bake the dough the next day, refrigerate it. The next day, bring the dough at room temperature for about 45 minutes to 1 hour and then proceed to baking.

Warm the olive oil for the topping in a small sauté-pan and add the garlic. Sauté slowly for about 1 to 2 minutes until the garlic is just soft, not brown. Combine the warm garlic oil and herbs in a small bowl. Let it come down to room temperature in about 30 minutes.

Step 4 – Shaping the dough and the final rise

Brush the baking sheet or the pizza pan generously with olive oil and sprinkle lightly with corn meal flour. Place the dough ball on a lightly floured work surface.

Use the heel of your hand or a rolling pin to press and flatten the dough until it is very thin, about ¼ inch thick. Lift and gently pull the dough, stretching it to fit into the pan. If the dough resists, let it rest for 5 minutes and then continue.

Cover gently with an oiled plastic wrap and let rise at room temperature until double in bulk, 30 minutes to 1 hour.

The difference between focaccia and pizza dough lies in the thickness and simplicity of the toppings.

Step 5 – Topping, baking, cooling and storage

Using your finger tips or knuckles, gently poke indentations all over the dough surface, about 2 inches apart. Drizzle the herb oil all over the dough, letting it pool in the indentations. Sprinkle lightly with salt.

If using a baking stone or a tile, place it on the lowest rack of the oven and preheat the oven to 230 degrees Celcius for 20 minutes. If you are not using the baking stone, then preheat the oven to 200 degrees.

Bake the bread for 30 to 35 minutes or until nicely browned.

Check the bottom half way through the baking time by lifting a side with a metal spatula to make sure the bottom is not too brown. If it is, slide another baking sheet of the same size, underneath the present one, known as double panning and continue baking. Let it cool in the pan itself or slide from the pan onto a cutting board to cut into wedges with a pizza wheel or a serrated bread knife.

Focaccia is best eaten the day it is baked. You can freeze it upto one month for storage purposes. When required, defrost, wrapped at room temperature and warm in the oven on the baking sheet before serving.

Baby Semolina Focaccia

These little focaccia, also called *Focaccine* are really fun to make since you get to make a mix-n-match pattern with toppings.

The dough is made with semolina paste flour. These free forms are great as appetisers with wine, while the pan focaccia are better served in wedges or slices.

Though you can top the dough with as many flavours as you like, still it is preferable to use 1 or 2 flavours for 1 focaccine, so as not to confuse the flavours. Moreover, the flavour of the focaccine bread should be the dominant one.

To make eight 6-inch or free-form rounds, you require: Bakeware: Two 11×17-inch baking sheets or eight 6-inch round cake pans, at least 1-inch deep.

Ingredients

- One recipe focaccia with the herbs and garlic dough with one and a half cups semolina flour substituted for one and a half cups of the all-purpose flour.
- Yellow cornmeal flour for sprinkling over the pan.
- Half cup good quality olive oil, for brushing the dough.

Choice of toppings

- Roasted red pepper strips or coarsely grounded red pepper
- Chopped fresh or roasted garlic
- Half or chopped olives
- Sliced fresh round juicy tomatoes
- Mushrooms sautéed
- Grilled egg plant slices
- Thinly sliced zucchini
- Cut up frozen or canned marinated artichoke hearts (defrosted and drained, if canned)
- Chopped or slivered oil-packed sun-dried tomatoes (drained). (Tomatoes dried through processing and preserved in oil)
- Slivered prosciutto
- Black olive paste
- Basil pesto (Basil sauce – mixture of salt, pepper, oil and basil leaves)
- Whole fresh basil, sage or flat leaf parsley leaves
- Freshly grated mozzarella cheese

Method

Place a baking stone on the lowest rack of the oven and pre-heat the oven to 232 degrees Celsius. If not using the stone, pre-heat the oven to 204 degrees Celsius for fifteen minutes.

Line the baking sheets with the parchment paper or brush the pans with oil and sprinkle with cornmeal flour. Prepare the dough to the end of step 3 without the topping (Given in the page 120).

To shape the dough, place the dough balloon at lightly floured work surface and divide into eight equal portions. Using the heel of your hand, press and flatten the dough portions into free-form rounds, about six inches in diameter. Lift and stretch the dough, stretching it to round oval shapes on the baking sheet or pressing it to fit into the pans.

Cover loose with plastic wrap and let rest at room temperature for 20 minutes.

Press your fingertips over the surface of the dough to dimple it and brush liberally with olive oil. Arrange the toppings in any manner. You can combine the toppings, paying attention to contrasting colours, shapes and complimentary flavours.

Bake the dough for about 15-20 minutes, or until golden on the top and browned on the bottom.

Serve immediately or cool on a rack. Focaccine taste better when eaten on the same day.

Though you can top the dough with as many flavours as you like, still it is preferable to use 1 or 2 flavours for 1 focaccine, so as not to confuse the flavours. Moreover, the flavour of the focaccine bread should be the dominant one.

Walnut Fougasse

Fougasse is the French version of focaccia and is often enriched with walnut oil and chopped fresh walnuts. Serve it in wedges with unsalted butter.

To make one rectangle or round flat bread to serve 8 people, you require:
Bakeware: One 11×17-inch baking sheet or 14-inch deep-dish pizza pan.

Ingredients

One recipe focaccia with herbs and garlic dough with one-third walnut oil substituted for the olive oil and 1 cup coarsely chopped walnut added while making the dough.

Method

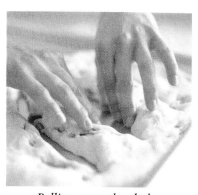

Pulling open the slashes in the fougasse

Line the baking sheet with parchment paper or brush the bottom and the sides of the baking sheet on pizza pan with oil.

Prepare the dough through the end of step 3 (page 120) (without the topping).

To shape the dough, use a rolling pin; roll out into a dough 9×12-inch rectangle or a 14-inch round, about half-inch thick. Transfer it to the pan. Let it rest, covered with oil plastic wrap, until double in bulk, 30 minutes to 1 hour. Pre-heat the oven to 204 degrees Celsius for about 15 minutes. With a sharp knife, cut three-inch diagonal slashes right through the bottom of the pan. Pull the slashes open lightly with your fingers. Bake for 30-35 minutes or until nicely browned. Let it cool in the pan or slide onto a cutting board to serve warm.

Wholewheat Focaccia with Tomatoes & Sage

Using wholewheat flour gives a very distinct flavour and taste to the flat bread.

To make one rectangular flat bread to serve about 10, you require:

Bakeware: One 11×17-inch baking sheet or a 12×15-inch ceramic baking sheet pan.

Ingredients

- One recipe focaccia with herbs and garlic made with fine wholewheat flour instead of all-purpose flour with 10 fresh sage leaves, chopped, added while mixing the dough.
- ¼ cup good quality olive oil, for brushing the dough.
- 6 fresh juicy tomatoes seeded and sliced.
- 10 fresh sage leaves
- Sea salt for sprinkling
- Olive oil for drizzling

Method

Laying the baking sheet with parchment paper, brush the bottom and sides of the ceramic baking sheet with olive oil.

Prepare the dough through the end of step 3 without the toppings (Given in the page 120). Place the dough ball on a lightly floured work surface and roll out with a rolling pin into a 10×15-inch rectangle. Lift it and stretch it to fit into the pan. Let it rest, covered with oil plastic wrap, until double in bulk, for about 45 minutes.

Dimple the dough and brush it with olive oil. Arrange the tomato slices on the top and dot with the fresh sage leaves, with the stems pressed in the dough. Sprinkle with salt and drizzle with olive oil.

Preheat the oven to 203 degrees Celsius for about 20 minutes. Bake the dough for about 25-30 minutes, or until nicely browned. Let it cool on the pan itself or slide onto a cutting board and serve warm.

Grilled flat bread with herbs and cheese

To make 8 round flat bread.
Note: Baking bread outdoors over a charcoal or aromatic wood fire gives a unique flavour to the flat bread.

Ingredients

- One recipe focaccia with herbs and garlic dough
- ¾ cups chopped fresh basil; marjoram, sage, summer savoury, rosemary or parsley
- 1-cup olive oil
- Olive oil cooking spray
- Branches of rosemary, thyme or lavender
- 350 grams smoked mozzarella cheese (Amul)
- Extra-virgin olive oil, for dipping

Method

Prepare the dough through the end of step 3 without toppings (Given in the page 120).

To shape the dough, turn it out onto a lightly worked surface and divide it into 8 equal portions. Using a rolling pin, roll each portion out to an 8-inch free form round. Sprinkle each with herbs and use the rolling pin to press the herbs into the dough surface. Drizzle each round with 1 tablespoon olive oil and transfer the round onto an aluminium foil or parchment paper. Sprinkle again with herbs and oil. Repeat the same with other rounds, stacking the flat breads on their foils to store. Let the rounds rest for about 45 minutes.

Focaccia is often topped with only olive oil and salt. Toppings like mushroom, cheese and onions are meant to be scattered lightly as flavour enhancers and not as generously like pizza toppings. Flat breads can also be enhanced with sugar, honey, spices, dried and fresh fruit.

Meanwhile prepare an outdoor charcoal or wood fire in half of the grill. When the coals are covered with gray ash, throw a few herb branches on top of the coals for extra aroma while grilling. You can even grill on your gas stove.

Pre-heat the burner on a high flame, then lower the flame while baking the second side. Spray a clean grill rack with olive oil cooking spray and place it four inches above the fire. Flip the flat bread onto the hot side of the grill and remove the foil immediately. Grill as many types of bread as will fit at one go.

Cook for 1 to 2 minutes, or until firm and puffed, then turn once with metal tongs to grill the other side, moving the flat bread to the area of the grill with indirect heat, for about 7 to 8 minutes. Drizzle with more olive oil and top with a layer of cheese. Transfer from the grill to a cutting board. Cut into quarters.

Serve warm in a basket with olive oil for dripping, if desired.

Cheese-stuffed Focaccia

This is one of the unique ways to shape focaccia. The dough is rolled out and filled with mild semi-soft cheese, one that is firm enough to slice or grate, yet melts into a buttery soft mass on heating.

Press edges of top and bottom rounds together to seal

To make 1 flat bread serving 6 to 8, you require:
Bakeware: One 11×17-inch rectangular baking sheet or 12-inch round pizza pan.

Ingredients

- One recipe focaccia with herbs and garlic dough
- 350 gms of cheese, sliced or coarsely grated.
- 1/3 cup finely grated parmesan cheese
- 3 tablespoons olive oil for brushing

Method

Line the baking sheet with parchment paper or brush the pan with oil. Prepare the dough through the end of step 3 without the topping (Given in the page 120).

To shape the dough, place the dough ball on a lightly worked surface and divide into two equal portions. Using the rolling pin, roll out one portion to a 10-inch round and about 1/8-inch thick. Transfer it on the pan. Take care not to tear the dough or else the cheese will leak out during baking.

Spread the round with a grated or sliced cheese and sprinkle with the finely grated Parmesan cheese, leaving a 1½-inch border. Brush the edges of the dough with water. Roll out the remaining portion of the dough on lightly floured surface. Fold it in half and cut a small hole in the centre of the folded edge to make a vent for the steam to escape. Unfold and place on top of the first round with filling. Press the edges together and crump to seal. Brush the top with olive oil and cover with a clean, damp, tea-towel and let rise at room temperature until double in bulk, for about 30 minutes to 1 hour.

Pre-heat the oven to 232 degrees Celsius for 20 minutes, if using the baking stone. If not using the baking stone, pre-heat the oven to 204 degrees Celsius.

Bake on the lowest rack for about 10-15 minutes; or until golden brown on top, yet a little bit soft. Cut the wedges and serve hot.

coffee cake

Though coffee cake is usually made once in a while for special occasions rather than on a daily basis, it holds a special place in every baker's baking list. Coffee cakes blend the techniques of yeast baking with those of creating intricate shapes, of making luscious filling to be enclosed in the dough, and of experimenting textured toppings.

Classic coffee cakes are 3 times higher in fat, eggs and sugar than everyday loaves, giving them a refined and delicious taste and luxurious texture. Attention to timing is often necessary, since glazes are applied to dough of different temperatures and fillings must be of the correct consistency.

Coffee cakes are either eaten on their own or after a morning or early afternoon meal. Each bite is a luxury, soft and sweet. The cakes speak of quality and care; that this is special food and that a little extra something went into its preparation. Coffee cakes used to be an integral part of the afternoon tea, which was a type of ritual for all classes of society in Europe. Many royal families still observe this tradition.

These coffee cake doughs are no harder to manipulate than regular bread doughs, although they need less kneading and more rising time. When you go to shape the dough, if it rises even a little bit, just let it rest and relax for 10 minutes and then proceed. With this little rest period, the dough will easily take shape. If you are working with half or a quarter of the dough, cover the rest of the portion with a clean dish-towel or a piece of plastic wrap. Do not worry if it rises a bit while you are working. When brushing the dough with butter or filling, always leave ½-inch border all the way around the rolled out dough to prevent the filling from oozing out during the shaping and baking. Moreover, sweet doughs need to be baked at a lower temperature than regular breads, since they tend to burn at high temperatures.

Most coffee cakes are very old-fashioned, encouraging the addition of spices, nuts and dry fruits. They are often seasonal incorporating chocolates, pumpkins, lemons, apples, dry fruits and nuts in winters and fresh fruits, extracts and creamy cheese in summers. Fillings made of poppy seed, cherry, prunes, and almonds can be prepared a day ahead and refrigerated.

An important element in finishing many coffee breads is the crumb topping called STREUSEL, which means litter or dust in German. Sugar, flour, butter and sometimes nuts or spices, are mixed together into a mass of clumps, which are distributed over the coffee cake before baking. The proportions in Streusel vary slightly, giving a crisp, thin topping or a thick, soft crumb topping. This type of finishing touch has been popular for centuries.

Use good heavy baking sheets for baking free-form logs, fruit strips, crescents, tea-rings and pan crumb cakes. For round cakes, use spring-form pans, which are doubly convenient, because you don't have to invert a delicate cake to turn it out and can serve it directly from the spring-form bottom placed on a plate.

You can also serve a cake directly out of decorative porcelain baking dish, oven-proof glass or earthenware baking dish, giving an aesthetic look to the coffee cake.

Baking of a Coffee Cake in the Morning

Since the allure of coffee cake, warm and just out of the oven, is hard to beat, many bakers mix, rise and shape a cake the day before serving, then "bake it off" in the morning before breakfast or brunch. To follow this method, loosely cover the shaped cake with plastic wrap and let rise at room temperature for about 30 minutes. Then cover the unbaked cake with a double layer of plastic wrap, leaving a bit of room for expansion, and refrigerate overnight. The next morning, take out the dough and let the dough come down at room temperature.

Pre-heat the oven for about 20 minutes and then bake as directed in the recipe.

Freezing Baked Coffee Cakes

When the coffee cake is completely cooled, place it in a single layer in a large, shallow plastic container with an air-tight lid, or in a double layer of plastic freezing bag. For larger cakes, wrap it in a layer of plastic wrap and then in a layer of heavy-duty foil. You can store these cakes up to three months in the freezer. It is preferable to frost or dust cakes with powdered sugar after they are defrosted.

If you are in a hurry, a frozen coffee cakes can be defrosted and warmed in the oven. Or just place the wrapped frozen cake on the counter and let it defrost by itself for a few hours before re-heating. Then place the frozen coffee cake on a parchment-lined baking sheet. Tent it with a piece of foil sprayed with vegetable oil to prevent sticking. Tuck the ends of the foil under the coffee cake. Warm it in the oven at 300 degrees Celsius for about 10 to 20 minutes, depending upon the size of the cake. Serve it warm.

Prune Butter Coffee Cake

This is a simple name for a divine Viennese-style coffee cake. The little dumplings are filled with a home-made prune paste or thick purple plum jam spread, that makes them quite delicious and tempting to eat.

To make two 10-inch round coffee cans, you require: Bakeware: Two 10-inch spring form pans.

Ingredients

For Coffee Cake Sweet Bread Dough

- ¼ cup warm water (40-45 degrees Celsius)
- 1 tablespoon active dry yeast
- 1/3 cup sugar
- 5¾-6¼ cups all-purpose flour
- 1½ teaspoons salt
- ½ cup warm milk (40-45 degrees Celsius)
- 1 cup sour cream

- 3 large eggs
- Finely grated zest of 1 lemon or orange
- 8 tablespoons unsalted butter at room temperature cut into small pieces.

For Prune Butter Filling

- 9 ounces (1 ounce = 28 gms) pitted dried prunes
- ¼ cup sugar
- 3 tablespoons fresh orange juice
- 2 tablespoons unsalted butter
- 1 large egg

For Cinnamon Sugar

- 2/3 cup sugar
- 1 teaspoon ground cinnamon
- 1 tablespoon melted unsalted butter

Method

Follow the steps given below carefully.

Step 1 – Mixing the Dough

Assemble the ingredients and equipment around your work surface. Pour the warm water into a small bowl. Sprinkle the yeast and a pinch of sugar over the surface. Stir to dissolve and let stand at room temperature until foamy for about 10 minutes. The batter can be made by hand and also by mixer.

To make by hand

Combine 1½ cups of flour, the remaining sugar and the salt in a large bowl. Make a well and add the milk, sour cream, eggs and the zest in the centre. Using a balloon or dough whisk beat until smooth for about 1 minute. Add the yeast mixture and beat vigorously for about 1 minute more. Add 1 cup more flour and beat for 1 minute. Switch over to a wooden spoon when the dough clogs the whisk. Add the butter pieces and beat until they have blended well. Add the remaining flour, half cup at a time, until soft, shaggy dough that pulls away from the sides of the bowl is formed. The dough should make a very soft ball, pull away from the sides of the bowl and roll around. The dough should be softer than the bread dough. Do not add too much flour; this is very delicate and moist dough.

To make by a mixer

If using a heavy-dury electric mixer with paddle attachment, place 1½ cups of the flour, remaining sugar and salt in the work bowl. Make a well and add the milk, sour cream, eggs and the zest in the centre. Beat until smooth on medium-low speed for about 1 minute. Add the yeast mixture and beat for 1 minute more. Stop the machine and add 1 cup flour. Beat for 1 minute. Add the butter pieces and beat on low speed until they have mixed well. Stop the machine or use the flour guard, when adding the flour to keep it from jumping out of the bowl. Add the remaining flour half cup at a time, until soft, smooth dough that just clears the sides of the bowl. Switch to the dough hook when the dough thickens, about two-thirds through the process of adding the flour, and knead for about 5 minutes on medium-high speed.

Soft coffee cake dough after kneading

Step 2 – Kneading

Using a plastic dough card, turn the dough out onto a lightly floured work surface. Knead until smooth, till the

Dipping dough pockets in cinnamon sugar

dough is just able to hold its own shape, under 1 minute for a machine-mixed dough and for 3-4 minutes for the hand-mixed dough. Dust with flour only 1 tablespoon at a time, just enough to prevent the dough from sticking to your hands and the work surface. The dough should be very smooth, with a definite soft elastic quality, not stiff and should be able to hold its own shape.

Step 3 – Rising and making the filling

Place the dough bowl in a greased deep container, turn it over to grease the top also, and cover it loosely with a plastic wrap. If using a mixer, you can put on the lid and let the dough dry in the work bowl. Let it rise at room temperature until double in bulk, for about 2½-3 hours. Do not allow the dough to rise more than double; it has a tendency to tear and the baked loaf will not be as fluffy. The dough must also be refrigerated at this point from 2-4 hours. Do not punch or deflate the dough.

To make the prune filling, combine the prunes, sugar, orange juice and butter in a small saucepan. Cook and cover over low heat, until soft and thick, for about 10 minutes. Cool slightly. Make a puree of this mixture in a food processor or with a hand blender. Let it cool down to room temperature. This puree can be made a day ahead and refrigerated covered.

Step 4 – Shaping the dough and final rise

If the dough has been refrigerated, let it stand at room temperature for about 2 hours before shaping. Butter the baking pans generously. Beat the egg and mix into the prune butter. Place the melted butter in a shallow bowl and combine the cinnamon and sugar in another shallow bowl.

Turn the dough out onto a lightly floured work surface, so that the dough deflates. Divide the dough in half and with the rolling pin, roll each portion into a 12-inch square. With a knife or a pastry wheel, divide into 3-inch squares (16 little squares from each large square). Place a generous teaspoon of the filling in the centre of each square. Fold the four corners into the centre and pinch together to seal in the filling. Dip the smooth end of each square in the melted butter and then into the cinnamon sugar just to coat the smooth surface. Place each square side by side, just touching each other in the baking pan. Cover each pan loosely with a plastic wrap and let rise at room temperature until almost double in bulk, in about 45 minutes.

Step 5 – Baking, cooling and storage

Pre-heat the oven at 175 degrees Celsius for about 20 minutes. Bake the small cakes at the lower third of the oven for 35-40 minutes or until the loaves are deep golden brown on the top and the sides have slightly shrunk away from the sides of the pan. Place the pans on a cooling rack and remove the spring from sides. Using a long spatula or knife, loosen the bottom and slide the cakes off the pan. Let cool on a cooling rack to room temperature and cut into wedges.

You can store the coffee cakes in the refrigerator, wrapped in a plastic food storage bag upto three days or you can keep them in the freezer compartment upto three months for longer storage.

Cream Cheese Breads

This is a delicate, creamy filling that melts deliciously in the mouth. The false plait is by far the most favourable coffee cake shape; it encloses the filling perfectly.

Ingredients

For sweet cheese filling

- 1 pound (450 gms.) cream cheese, at room temperature
- ½ cup sugar
- 2 tablespoons all-purpose flour
- 1 egg
- 2 tablespoons pure vanilla extract
- Grated zest of 1 lemon or orange
- 1 recipe coffee cake sweet bread dough

For glaze

- ¼ cup sugar
- 1 tablespoon evaporated skimmed milk
- 2 tablespoons fresh lemon or orange juice

Method

To make the filling

Beat the cream cheese, sugar and flour with an electric mixer until smooth. Add the egg, vanilla and the zest and beat until smooth. You can cover and refrigerate this mixture, until needed. It can be prepared one day ahead of baking. The filling makes about 3½ cups.

Line the baking sheet with the parchment paper. Prepare the dough to the end of step 3 without the filling (Given in the page 136).

To shape the coffee cakes, divide the risen dough into two equal portions. Using a rolling pin, roll out each portion on a lightly floured work surface to a 9×16-inch rectangle. Transfer to one of the parchment-lying baking sheets. Spread half of the cheese filling down the centre third of each piece of the dough, leaving one-inch border on the top and bottom edges. With a sharp knife, cut strips slightly on the diagonal,

2 inches apart, almost upto the filling. Starting at the top, fold the strips alternately over the filling. If there is any excess dough left at the end, tuck it under the adjacent strips. Cover loosely with plastic wrap and let rise at room temperature, until almost double, for about 45 minutes. Repeat the process for the second portion of the dough.

Pre-heat the oven to 175 degrees Celsius, for about 20 minutes. Meanwhile prepare the glaze. Mix the sugar, milk and juice with a whisk in a small bowl, until smooth. Brush gently over the top surfaces of the bread with a pastry brush. Bake the dough in the lower third of the oven at 175 degrees Celsius for about 30-35 minutes, or until the bread is golden brown and the filling is set. Remove the bread from the pan carefully and cool them on a cooling rack.

Nut Rolls

Nut rolls are a craze in Hungary, and are homemade for all occasions. They are known as BEIGLI, and carry a long tradition.

To make three twists, you require:
Bakeware: One 11×17-inch baking sheet

Ingredients

For nut paste

- 2 cups walnuts
- ½ cup light brown sugar
- 1 teaspoon ground cinnamon
- ½ teaspoon ground all spices
- ¼ cup hot evaporated skimmed milk
- 1 tablespoon unsalted butter
- 2 teaspoons vanilla extract
- 1 recipe coffee cake sweet bread dough
- 1 egg mixed with water, for glaze
- 1/3 cup powdered sugar, for dusting

Method

Filling

To make the filling, place the walnuts, brown sugar, cinnamon, and all spices in the work bowl of the food processor. Process until the nuts are ground. Combine the milk, butter and vanilla extract in a cup. Stir until the butter is melted. With the machine running, pour this mixture in through the feed tube until a thick paste is formed. Set aside. This mixture will measure about 1½ cups.

Line the baking sheet with the parchment paper. Prepare the dough through the end of step 3 without the fillings (Given in the page 136).

To shape the dough, divide the risen dough into three equal portions. Using the rolling pin, roll out each portion on a lightly floured work surface to a 10 × 12-inch rectangle. Spread each portion with 1/3 of the nut paste, leaving a one-inch border on the top and bottom edges. Roll up in jellyroll fashion from the long edge, pinch the bottom seam to seal and pinch the ends and tuck under. Arrange each roll side by side on one of the parchment-lined baking sheets. Flatten slightly by pressing with your hands.

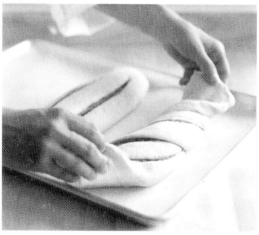

Holding an end in each hand, twist to make a twisted rope

With the sharp knife, cut two parallel slits lengthwise, two inches apart, leaving the roll uncut about two inches from each end. Holding an end in each hand, twist the ends in opposite direction (like twisting a rope), very carefully.

The slits will open, showing the filling. Cover loosely with plastic wrap and let rise at room temperature, until almost double about 45 minutes.

Pre-heat the oven to 175 degrees Celsius, for about 20 minutes. Meanwhile, beat the egg and water in a small bowl with a fork until foamy. Using a pastry brush, gently brush the tops of the loaf with this glaze. Bake the rolls in the lower third of the oven, until the bread is golden brown and the filling is set, for about 25-30 minutes.

Remove from the pan carefully and transfer to a cooling rack. After the nut rolls have cooled completely, place the powdered sugar in a fine mesh sieve, and shaking the sieve, dust the top of the nut rolls with sugar.

Saffron Coffee Bread

Saffron coffee bread is one of the most traditionally flavoured and coloured sweet bread of the British Isles.

To make one cake, about 12 slices, you require:
Bakeware: One 12-cup (10- inch) non-stick Bundt pan

Ingredients

- ½ cup sliced almonds, for sprinkling
- ¼ cup powdered sugar
- Fresh berries for serving
- One recipe coffee cake sweet bread dough made with 1/3 teaspoon saffron threads (or 1/8 teaspoon ground saffron) soaked in the warm milk for 10 minutes before mixing and 1¼ cups dried currants added when mixing the dough

Method

Generously butter the Bundt pan. Arrange the almonds on the bottom. Prepare the dough through the end of step 3 (Given in the page 136). To shape the dough, turn out the rising dough onto the work surface. Using the palm of your hand, roll the dough back and forth to make a fat, compact cylinder, 16-18 inches long.

Lay it in the buttered pan with the two ends touching and press the dough evenly in the bottom, adjusting it to lie evenly in the pan, no more than 2/3 full.

Cover loosely with plastic wrap and let rise at room temperature until the cake reaches the rim of the pan and has almost doubled, in about 45-60 minutes.

Pre-heat the oven to 175 degrees Celsius for about 20 minutes. The dough is to be baked in the lower third position of the oven.

After placing the dough in the oven, check after 30 minutes, and if the top is browning too quickly, tent the dough with a piece of aluminium foil and then bake again. Bake the dough for about 20-25 minutes more.

Lifting sections and turning on their sides

Place the bread on a cooling rack for about 5 minutes to cool. If the sides are too pale, place on a baking sheet and bake for another 3-8 minutes. Invert on a wire rack to cool completely before slicing. Dust with powdered sugar and serve in thick slices with fresh berries on the sides.

Orange Coffee Crescent

This is a variation of a Swedish tea ring, in which a log of filled dough is cut at intervals and turned flat to expose the fillings. Not only is this shape attractive, it is elegant enough to be a table centrepiece.

To make two cakes, you require:
Bakeware: Two 11×17-inch baking sheet

Ingredients

For orange-raisin filling

- One whole orange
- One cup sugar
- 1¼ cup chopped almonds
- 1½ cup golden raisins
- ¼ cup chopped candied orange peel

For rum butter

- 4 tablespoons butter
- 1 tablespoon dark rum
- One recipe coffee cake sweet bread dough
- One egg beaten with one tablespoon milk and
- ¼ teaspoon vanilla extract for the glaze

Method

Filling

To make the filling, using a small pairing knife, cut the peel of the orange, taking care not to get too much of the white pith. Place the peel in a food processor with the sugar and process until finely chopped. Combine the orange sugar with the almonds, raisins and candied peel in a bowl. Melt together with butter and rum.

Line the baking sheet with the parchment paper. Prepare the dough through the end of step 3 (Given in the page 136).

To shape the coffee cakes, turn out the raisin dough onto a work surface and divide into two equal portions. Using a rolling pin, roll each portion into a 9×14-inch rectangle, about ¼-1/3 inches thick. Brush each portion with half of the rum and butter, and sprinkle evenly with half of the filling, leaving a half-inch border all the way round. Roll up from the long edge, jellyroll fashion, pinching the long seam to seal but leaving the ends open. Carefully transfer back roll to a baking sheet and curve into half moon, semi-circle or horseshoe – 'U' shape. Using kitchen shears, cut two-thirds of the way, from the outer edge towards the centre, at 2-inch intervals (about 8 cuts). Lift each section and turn it onto its side to lie flat on the baking sheet. Consequently, the filling will be exposed on the top. Turn all the sections in the same direction. Cover loosely with plastic wrap and let rise at room temperature until puffy in about 1½ hours.

Pre-heat the oven to 175 degrees Celsius for about 20 minutes. Brush the top of the cake with the egg glaze, and bake one cake at a time. Bake the dough at the lower third of the oven, until golden brown and firm to touch, for about 30-35 minutes. Bake the second crescent in the same manner. Slide the parchment paper of the baking sheet with the cake on it, onto a wire rack to cool.

Poppy seed streusekuchen

Crunch poppy seeds are such a favourite ingredients in Austro-Hungarian and Polish baking, that they are a must in most baked items. Since poppy seeds need to be ground, which can be a hassle, you can also use canned poppy seed filling.

To make two round coffee cakes, you require:
Bakeware: Two 12-inch spring form pans or regular cake pans.

Ingredients

- One recipe coffee cake sweet bread dough
- Two 12-ounce (1 ounce = 28 gms) poppy seed filling, crumbled

For crumb topping

- 2½ cups, all-purpose flour
- 1 cup powdered sugar
- Two teaspoons baking powder
- Two teaspoons ground cardamom
- ½ teaspoon ground cinnamon
- 1 cup unsalted butter, chilled and cut into pieces
- 1/3 powdered sugar for dusting

Method

Generously butter the pans. Prepare the dough through the end of step 3 (Given in the page 136) (without the filling).

To shape the dough, divide the risen dough into two equal portions. On a lightly floured work surface, pat each portion into a flat disc. Place in the buttered pans to let rest for 10 minutes, covered loosely with plastic wrap. Pat the dough out to evenly fit the bottom of the pans.

To make the crumb topping, combine the flour, sugar, baking powder, cardamom, and cinnamon in a small bowl or the cup of the food processor. Cut the butter in small pieces and add them to the flour mixture. Mix coarsely till dry coarse crumbs are formed. Do not overmix or the crumbs will clump.

Sprinkle each portion of the dough with half of the poppy seed filling, leaving a half-inch border around the edge. Divide the crumb topping in half, and cover the filling

To make the crumb topping, combine the flour, sugar, baking powder, cardamom and cinnamon in a small bowl or the cup of the food processor. Cut the butter in small pieces and add them to the flour mixture. Mix coarsely till dry coarse crumbs are formed. Do not overmix or the crumbs will clump.

completely with an even layer. Cover loosely with plastic wrap and let rise a room temperature until puffy; about 25 minutes.

Pre-heat the oven to 190 degrees Celsius for about 20 minutes. Bake at the lower third of the oven, for 25-30 minutes or until the cake is golden brown and a cake tester comes out clean.

Transfer the pan to a cooling rack, remove the sides of the spring from pan and cool. Dust with powdered sugar.

Serve warm or at room temperature, cut as wedges.

Spiced Apple-cheese crumb cake

This is the coffee cake to be made to serve at a party. It is a great favourite with folks. The cake has both the fruit filling and a cheese one, and then is finished with a crumb top.

It is essential that the recipe be baked in a baking sheet with a one-inch rim.

To make 1 large rectangle cake to serve about 15 people, you require:
Bakeware: One 11×17-inch baking sheet

Ingredients

One recipe of coffee cake sweet bread dough

For apple filling

- 4 pounds (1¾ kg) green apples, peeled, cored and thinly sliced.
- ¼ cup apple juice or water
- ½ cup granulated sugar
- 1 tablespoon fresh lemon juice
- Grated zest of one lemon
- 1 teaspoon ground cinnamon
- 4 tablespoons unsalted butter

For vanilla cheese filling

- 700 gms cream cheese at room temperature
- ½ cup granulated sugar or honey
- 3 eggs
- 1½ tablespoons pure vanilla extract

For cinnamon crum topping

- 1 cup all-purpose flour
- 2/3 cup light brown sugar
- 2 teaspoons ground cinnamon
- 10 tablespoons unsalted butter, chilled and cut into pieces

Method

Prepare the dough through the end of step 3 (Given in the page 136) (without the filling). While the dough is rising, prepare the apple filling, cheese filling and crumb top.

To make the apple filling, place all the ingredients in a large, heavy non-reactive saucepan. Bring to a boil. Then reduce the heat to medium-low and cook uncovered, until the liquid is evaporated, the mixture is thick and the apples are soft. Keep stirring frequently to avoid sticking for about 15 minutes. Set aside to cool completely. This filling can be prepared one day ahead and refrigerated. After taking it out from the refrigerator, bring the filling down to room temperature before using.

To make the cheese filling, beat the cheese, sugar or honey eggs and vanilla with an electric mixture until smooth and creamy, for about two minutes. This mixture can also be prepared one day ahead and refrigerated until needed.

To make the crumb top, combine the flour, brown sugar and cinnamon in a small bowl or food processor. Cut the butter in small pieces and add it to rest of the mixture. Mix till dry coarse crumbs are formed. Again, the topping can be prepared in advance and refrigerated.

Pre-heat the oven at 175 degree Celsius for about 20 minutes. Lay the baking sheet with the parchment paper and grease the sides of the baking pan. To shape the dough, turn the risen dough out onto the lightly floured work surface and divide in half. Using a rolling pin, roll out half of the dough into a 13×19-inch rectangle. Fit it into the pan, pressing to fit upside. With a large spatula, spread the entire cheese filling over the dough in an even layer, leaving a half-inch border all around. Spread the entire apple filling over the cheese filling. Roll out the remaining half of the dough to a 12×18-inch rectangle. Gently set this rolled out portion over the fruit-layered portion and tuck the edges down along the insides of the pan to contain the filling. Crimp the edges as made, while making 'gunjia'. Sprinkle evenly with the crumb topping and set aside to rest at room temperature for 15 minutes.

Bake for 35-40 minutes, or until golden brown and firm to the touch. Place the pan on the rack to cool. Serve in squares cut from the pan, warm or at room temperature.

glossary

A

Allspice: Mixture of nutmeg, cinnamon, javitri and black pepper.
Aniseed: Saunf
Artichoke: A plant with large thistle-like flower heads.
Aubergine: Baingan

B

Barley: Jaun
Basil: Tulsi
Bay leaves: Tejpatta
Black cardamom: Badi Elaichi
Black onion seeds: Kalonji
Blackberry: Jamun

C

Caraway seeds: Shahi Jeera
Carom seeds: Ajwain
Castor sugar: Pisi Cheeni
Celery seeds: Seeds from the wild Indian celery called Lovage.
Cinnamon: Dalchini
Cloves: Laung
Coloccasia: Arbi
Currants (black): Munacca

D

Dates: Khajoor
Dill seed: Suwa bhaji seed from the Dill plant. A culinary and medicinal herb of the parsley family.
Dill weed: Feathery green leaves from the dill plant.

F

Fennel seeds: Badi Saunf
Fig: Anjeer

G

Gramflour: Besan
Gooseberry: Amla

Hazelnut: Small bush or tree bearing hard-shelled nuts of yellowish brown colour. Nuts from the tree of the Oak family.

Lovage: Large, dark green celery like leaves.
Lemon Peel: Yellow outer skin of lemon which is grated. It is also called lemon zest.
Linseed: Alsi

Mace: Javitri. Bright red outer covering of nutmeg seed that turns yellow-orange when dried.
Marjoram: Oval, inch long leaves. Member of the mint/ oregano family.
Molasses: Khand. Thick syrup drained from sugar in the process of refining.

Nutmeg: Jaiphal

Oats: Jaie
Olives: Jaitoon
Orange peel: Outer skin of orange which is grated. Also called orange zest.
Oregano: Member of the mint family, related to thyme, a culinary herb.

Parsley: Ajmoda. Herb with crinky aromatic leaves used to season and garnish foods. Looks similar to Coriander leaves
Pinenuts: Tilkoja
Plum: Aloocha. Small sweet, oval, fleshy fruit, reddish-purple in colour.
Poppy seeds: Khuskhus. Seeds from the poppy plant.
Prunes: Dried plums.

Rock Salt: Kala Namak
Rosemary: Mehandi. Silver-green, needle-shaped leaves, member of the mint family. An evergreen fragrant shrub.

Rye: Type of cereal found in some parts of Europe, from which bread is made.

S

Saffron: Kesar
Sage: Narrow oval, grey-green leaves. A kind of aromatic herb like Tulsi.
Sago: Sabudana
Savory: Herb related to the mint family. Two types: Summer and winter.
Semolina: Suji
Sesame: Til
Star anise: Badiyan/Chakriphool. Dried, reddish brown fruit.
Sunflower seeds: Black elongated seeds like tilgoja.

T

Tarragon: A culinary herb with narrow, pointed, dark green leaves.
Thyme: Bush with grey-green leaves. Member of the mint family.

Nutritious Mushroom Recipes

—*Prabhjot Mundhir*

'Foods can make or break you' is an established fact. That is why it is important to include the mushroom – one of nature's greatest wonder foods – in one's diet. Some varieties have anti-cholesterol and antibiotic properties. The common variety is full of high quality protein as well as B vitamins. With its irresistible taste, exotic flavour and rich aroma, the mushroom's delicious dishes are a healthy alternative to meat dishes. Keeping Indian tastes in mind, the author has innovated some easy-to-follow recipes.

The book contains recipes on starters, soups, salads and dishes for the main course. Some of the starters and quick stir-fried vegetable dishes of mushrooms are just ideal for tiffin boxes of children, working women and other office-goers. Most ingredients used are easily available. To retain natural taste and flavour, spices are used sparingly. Unlike some cookery books that are merely compilations, all the recipes presented here are tried, tested or innovated by the author and would be just ideal for daily meals. Besides, these dishes can easily be a part of any Indian or Continental menu set for special occasions too. In short, mushrooms used in everyday cooking will help maintain the good health of your loved ones.

Small Size • Pages: 128 (Coloured)
Price: Rs. 96/- • Postage: Rs. 15/-